THE NEW AMERICAN
Family

Dr. Mary Ann Artlip
James A. Artlip
Dr. Earl S. Saltzman

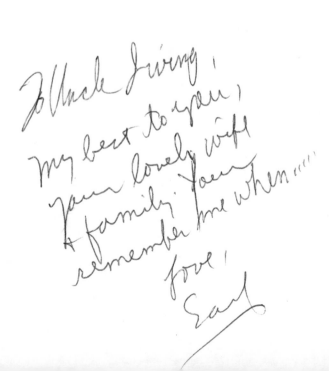

To Uncle Irving,
my best to you,
your lovely wife
+ family. You
remember me when....
love!
Earl

THE NEW AMERICAN

Family

Dr. Mary Ann Artlip
James A. Artlip
Dr. Earl S. Saltzman

STARBURST PUBLISHERS
TM

P.O. Box 4123, Lancaster, Pennsylvania 17604

Mary Ann Artlip, Ph.D. in English, is on the faculty of the University of Houston. James A. Artlip, MBA, CPA, is a senior systems designer with Exxon Chemical Americas. Earl S. Saltzman, Ph.D. in Psychology, is the director of the Saltzman Center for Structured Communication in Houston, Texas, and is the author of several audio tapes on marriage, parenting, and child discipline.

To schedule Author appearances write:
Author Appearances, Starburst Promotions, P.O. Box 4123
Lancaster, Pennsylvania 17604 or call (717) 293-0939

Credits:
Cover art by Bill Dussinger

THE NEW AMERICAN FAMILY

First Printing, February 1993

ISBN: 0-914984-44-6
Library of Congress Catalog Number 92-81392

Printed in the United States of America

Dedication

To Our Children:
Brad and *Heidi Frahm*
Mark and *Jilian Artlip*
Beverly, Frank, and *David Saltzman*

Acknowledgments

Many people helped us with this book, and our greatest pleasure, now that we have finally finished it, is in being able to say "thank you" to them. Our special gratitude goes to the hundreds of parents and stepparents across the United States who took part in our research. Vickie Black-Lewis, Jim Lewis, Judy Dowler, Gene and Kim Randall, and George Cauthen were especially helpful in supporting our project.

Every idea in our book was discussed with Dr. Gerald Motz of the Saltzman Center, and our work benefited greatly from his insights and observations.

We would also like to express our appreciation to our families and our colleagues—Resanne Saltzman, Myldred Wilson, Charles and Elaine Artlip, the staff of the Saltzman Center, Dr. Russell Meyer of the University of Houston-Downtown, and the staff of the University of Houston Foundations Program: Dr. Helen Allen, Dominique Dominguez, Patricia Fadely, Homer Johnson, Doris Lott, and Jocelyn Mann. Special thanks go to Dr. Peter Levine and Robert Scott for their continued encouragement.

We are also very grateful to Ellen Hake and David Robie for sharing our vision and for supporting us in so many ways.

Contents

The Rose

It's the heart afraid of breaking
that never learns to dance.
It's the dream afraid of waking
that never takes the chance.
It's the one who won't be taken
who cannot seem to give,
And the soul afraid of dying
that never learns to live.

When the night has been too lonely
and the road has been too long,
And you think that love is only
for the lucky and the strong,
Just remember in the winter
far beneath the bitter snows
Lies the seed that with the sun's love
in the spring becomes the rose.

Our Story

When we married in 1983, the soloist sang "The Rose." Six of us walked down the aisle—Jim and Mary Ann, Jim's children (Mark and Jilian), and Mary Ann's children (Brad and Heidi). We all committed ourselves to "love and honor, respect and cherish" each other till death did us part. The six of us stood arm in arm at the altar as the organ played "The Wedding Song," and, afterwards, our friends and relatives told us that it had been a beautiful wedding.

At that moment, filled with happiness and high expectations, we became an "instant" family, *The New American Family,* one of 1800 new stepfamilies forming every day in the United States.[1]

The romance of the courtship had been exhilarating. The boys were both fourteen, and the girls were both eleven, so we had had good times together—playing games, going to the beach, sharing meals. We knew that we were becoming stepparents, but in our innocence (at age 39) we simply rationalized that stepchildren came with the partnership. In our deep abiding love for one another, we would be able to arrange all of the relationships in approximately the same way that we would arrange the furniture in our home.

Mary Ann and the girls had spent much of the time before the wedding shopping for matching dresses and shoes. Both boys were pleased when Jim bought them pin-striped Pierre Cardin three-piece suits. Our wedding invitations were personalized with our smiling pictures on the front, and we made plans to hold the reception at a resort hotel called "Adventureland." (We're not joking; that *was* the name.) Little did we realize then, the kind of "adventure" we would soon be facing.

Five years later, on Mother's Day, Jilian, now sixteen, sang "The Rose" at church and dedicated the song to her stepmother, Mary Ann. This time it was hard to keep from crying while listening to the song's powerful words. What a long "winter" living in a stepfamily turned out to be. Five years later we still didn't know if that seed was ever going to climb through the "bitter snows" and, "with the sun's love," become "the rose." The years had been far more difficult than we would ever have imagined. We were totally unprepared for the problems involved in merging two separate families. All of the children lived with us, but behind closed doors. We did not relate in any way like "The Brady Bunch," It was more like a battle zone!

In the time since we married, during our years of coping and learning, we have slowly come to realize that we are not alone. American men and women are remarrying at an astounding rate, and nearly 60% of the remarriages involve children under the age of eighteen.[2] Unfortunately, over half of those remarriages also end in divorce, with half of the "redivorces" occurring within five years.[3] Many other remarriages do not dissolve, but experience problems serious enough to threaten the marital relationship.

When couples who *have* dissolved their stepfamily bonds are later questioned as to the reasons for their "redivorce," most identify the problem as relationship conflicts with stepchildren.[4] Caring for, supporting, and nurturing someone else's children, even on a part-time basis, is an incredibly complex and difficult undertaking. When the children resist this effort, or, even worse, when the biological parent fails to involve himself/herself in solving problems in a positive manner, it can become almost impossible.

The Survey

Out of this background of personal experience and study, our survey on *The New American Family* evolved. We recognized that during the years since we've been married,we have learned valuable lessons about stepparenting, lessons which might be useful to others. From that base, we also realized that the lessons learned and the strategies adopted by large numbers of stepfamilies across the United States would be even more useful to men and women who were seeking guidance for stepfamily problems or who were contemplating a marriage or remarriage involving children.

The survey project was born! Its goals were to consider on a nationwide basis the following questions:

(1) What are the feelings of stepparents and spouses of stepparents about their situation?

(2) What are the actual problems involved in step-parenting?

(3) What are the causes of these problems?

(4) What solutions have American parents and stepparents developed to cope with the identified problems?

(5) What are some of the positive aspects of stepfamily living?

The study had two parts. The first part was a ten page questionnaire which included demographic, attitudinal, and factual questions for statistical evaluation, together with a number of open-ended requests for written elaboration in certain areas. More than 500 stepparents and parents from 47 states, and from all different kinds of stepfamily situations, responded to our request for help.

Some couples were newly married. Others had been together for more than twenty years. Some families had one child. One family had twenty children. A few families were on welfare. Several were wealthy. The extreme differences between the various family situations were fascinating to us—and a bit surprising. The common ground was the need and desire of all these individuals to share their experiences and feelings with other stepparents.

The second part of the study involved in-depth interviews with 50 of our respondents. These wonderful people gave us as much of their time as we needed, dug deeply into their own (sometimes painful) experiences, and freely offered answers to even the most personal questions. They felt that their disclosures and honesty could help others in the same situations. To them we are very grateful.

Dr. Earl S. Saltzman, a practicing psychologist, joined our project team shortly after we got the survey underway. This allowed us to approach our identification of stepfamily problems and successful strategies from several directions at once. Earl, through his ongoing counseling of stepfamilies at the Saltzman Center in Houston, Texas, is quite cognizant of the many difficulties which arise in blended families. Throughout this book, he provides specific advice and practical methods for dealing with these problems. He has also carefully reviewed the ideas and suggestions offered by the members of the stepfamilies included in our survey.

On a personal basis, the three of us approach stepfamily conflicts from the perspective of behavior patterns, stressing that parents and children can learn new positive strategies and important living skills. Many of our ideas are simple techniques which have been tested and which *do* work. As family members live together, change, and grow, they inevitably face problems, frustrations, and adjustments. If they could realize that this is only a predictable stage in the evolution of a new family and that it *can* be dealt with in productive ways, relationships could flourish rather than die as they too often do.

Our Goal

It is our hope that this book will provide guidance and growth, both for stepfamilies who wish to enhance the quality of their family relationships, and for anyone who is contemplating marrying into a child-related situation.

Building a successful stepfamily *is* a challenge. It is also one of the most potentially fulfilling and rewarding experiences you can ever undertake. Families "blend" with a lot of love. We want to see them work through their problems and keep that love burning.

"Brady Bunch" or "battle zone?" Our study shows that a new marriage, or remarriage with children involved, can be either. We hope that this guide will help you more clearly understand the hopes, the dreams, and the problems of stepfamilies in the United States today. We also hope that you, too, will learn about living and loving successfully within *The New American Family.*

Jim and Mary Ann Artlip
Earl S. Saltzman

Part One

Someday, My (Second) Prince Will Come

1

Great Expectations

"My husband and I were really in love. I wanted to marry a man who had children because I didn't think I could have any more. I had a son and he wanted brothers and sisters and a dad. My husband had custody of his children. One was four and one was six. I loved them, and I loved him. I wanted us to be one big happy family. I just thought he was the most wonderful person in the world. I thought we would be happy, you know? I thought we'd just walk off into the sunset. We had a wonderful honeymoon, thank heavens! For four days. But the day we came home, it was *reality*. His kids were brats. It's been quite a miserable situation. The first three or four years were a nightmare beyond belief. I exhausted myself trying to be all things to everybody, rescue everyone and create their happiness. I almost ended up in a mental hospital. I came so close to a breakdown. I barely caught myself in time. If anybody came to me who was contemplating marrying a man with children, I'd tell them not to do it."

Carolyn, 35, Utah

For many stepfamilies, great expectations and wonderful honeymoons, are, after marriage, transformed into "a nightmare beyond belief." A large number of stepparents urged us to tell our readers: "Don't do it. Don't even think about it. It's an absolute nightmare." For many blended families, this is true. For others, the experience is the opposite. The stepfamily unit can be immensely rewarding.

What makes the difference? One important factor in ensuring stepfamily success is the nature of your expectations. Make certain that they're realistic, not just fantasies. It's hard to tell just when it happens, but somewhere in the cycle after a man and woman say, "Let's get married," something changes. Expectations grow larger, and reality begins to blur.

Samuel Johnson once said that second marriages are the triumph of hope over experience. For many of us, this is true. Past experiences haven't been all that great. When our first marriages end, we're often disillusioned and discouraged. A second marriage offers us a second chance, and we want that chance so much. We're older now. We're wiser. We learned something from that first relationship. This time, we tell ourselves, it will all work out. This time it's going to be great! We remarry with high expectations and dreams.

When our grandparents married, they didn't expect too much: hard work, their share of problems, and, in the end, a sense of accomplishment. They weren't disappointed because they didn't expect all that much to begin with.

Today we ask a lot of marriage—not only the first time but the second or third time as well. "Having it all" is our byword: love, excitement, fulfillment, good incomes, great sex, and happiness.

We're optimistic about love. We believe that if we can imagine it, we can do it, live it, be it. We believe in the power of dreams over the grim realities of second marriage statistics. Many of us are very quickly disappointed. More than half of us get "redivorced." This does not have to happen. Once is more than enough to go through the pain and disappointment of divorce.

We began writing this book because we know from personal experience that building a successful blended family *is* possible. We also know that it isn't easy. If we could offer a magic potion, we would, but there are no potions, no simple solutions. We can, though, give you guidelines that can make the difference in whether your blended family succeeds or fails.

The couples who make it are usually the ones with a clear vision of their situation and a firm commitment to their marriage partner. Wicked stepmother myths are common in ancient fairy tales. "Cinderella," "Snow White," and "Hansel and Gretel" all gave stepmothers a bad name. Yet these fairy tales are not nearly as destructive as the "blended family" myths of the 1980's and 1990's. Stepfamily life will be much easier for you if you can come to terms with seven common "blended family" myths. If you can learn to view your family situation clearly, you will be less likely to feel disillusioned or victimized by the pressures of stepfamily living.

SEVEN MYTHS ABOUT REMARRIAGE WITH CHILDREN

Myth #1: *Second Marriages are Better Than First Marriages*

We have all seen the divorce statistics. We know that more than half of all second marriages end in divorce.[1] We know that second marriages fail both more frequently and more quickly than first marriages. Does that frighten us? Not really. Nearly all of our survey respondents felt, *before* they remarried, that: "This marriage will be BETTER!" After marriage, 57% of these same people, on at least one occasion, thought seriously of divorce. Nine percent of our respondents were, in fact, reporting on marriages which had already ended. Another three percent wrote to tell us that they had gone through a divorce or separation *during the course of the study!*

Greater experience and age do not necessarily help us cope any better. Building stepfamilies is harder than building first families. A number of studies have shown that the stress of living with stepchildren is cited as the main cause of the breakup in two-thirds of those marriages that end in redivorce.[2] This factor affects even the probability of remarriage. A divorced woman with no children has a 70% likelihood of remarriage while a woman with two children has only a 58% chance. With three or more children, the figure drops even lower.[3] Women with children are not only *less* likely to remarry but *more* likely to redivorce. The "second time around" is not easier. It's often tougher than the first time. Remarriage, with children, can be marvelously rewarding, but couples do begin their new marital relationship with extra risks.

Myth #2: *We'll All Love Each Other*

"Once we're a family, we'll all love each other." New stepparents express this hope so often. The reality is that "instant love" is one of the most destructive myths that stepparents can harbor. No matter what they do for their stepchildren, many stepmothers and stepfathers will not be loved. No matter how much they try, some stepparents will not be able to love their stepchildren. You can't magically force love to happen. Sometimes the feeling is simply not there.

In addition, the almost supernatural bonding that "glues" biological parents and children together can be a strong exclusionary force when stepparents come on the scene. Blood ties, even when tested by problems and emotional pain, are not easily broken.

Trying to suddenly be "mom" or "dad" just because a marriage has taken place can be a problem for adults and children alike. Yet many stepparents have an internal contract with themselves: this is the way things *should* be. When events do not come out in the "expected" way, the entire situation becomes a two-edged sword. Stepparents are hurt because their stepchildren don't love them like a parent, and, at the same time, they feel guilty because they don't love their stepchildren as strongly as they love their own children. In fact, they may not love their stepchildren at all! These stepparents then begin to criticize themselves: "This is not 'okay.' I AM NOT 'OKAY.' "

Stepparents usually have two thoughts in mind when they get trapped by this "instant love" myth. In addition to feeling that they *should* love their "new children," they firmly believe that they cannot fulfill their new parental role, cannot guide or discipline the children, unless they do so "with love." While love does make blended family living easier, it often takes time to develop. Stepparents should not become discouraged if it does not come at once. Love must be viewed as a goal, a seed, that will grow with nurturing care. Though stepchildren may resist loving gestures at first, stepparents can still have a positive influence on their stepchildren's lives. Camp counselors, teachers, and many other adults routinely guide and discipline young people without feeling a need to love them. It is often *the stepparent's need* to love and be loved—instantly!—that makes the overall situation difficult to handle.

Many of our survey responses illustrated the problems connected with the "instant love" myth. When Dawn married Gerald, she thought her love and caring for her stepchildren would automatically be returned.

"I thought if I was a loving, caring person his children would love me in return."

Dawn *was* a loving, caring person, but Gerald's three children did not love her in return. She found this very difficult to accept. She felt that she was endlessly loving, endlessly giving, but getting nothing back.

"It got worse and worse. The older girl nearly caused a divorce. They have learned to take everything they can get and give back NOTHING.

. . .They make me ANGRY at my husband for allowing them to HURT me. I'm a lot more cynical now—not as sweet or naive. I'm not sure these are positive changes; I know I don't like them."

Dawn, 36, Massachusetts

Dawn's emphasis on the words "nothing," "angry," and "hurt" reveal how much she wanted to love and be loved and how disillusioned and upset she is now.

One of the most difficult truths stepparents, especially stepmothers, have to face is the myth of "instant love." Half of the stepparents in our survey strongly expected this from their stepchildren. Most were disappointed.

When Karin married, she felt:

" . . . that everyone would be automatically happy together and that my stepchildren would love me right from the start."

After six years of marriage, Karin is bitterly hurt and has considered divorce a number of times. She feels her expectations for love were totally unrealistic.

"It's very painful. It makes you feel so rejected."

Karin, 28, South Carolina

The men in our survey were not as vehement, but they, too, often felt cheated. They expected more from these children (whom they often supported financially) than they usually received.

"You give a lot for little return."

William, 48, South Carolina

"You give a lot for little return" aptly describes what happens to many stepparents in the first weeks, months, and even years of stepfamily living. How should this problem be handled? When you give so much, isn't it fair to expect something positive in return?

Another stepparent, David, pared his expectations down to the basics:

". . . safe sex and someone to keep my back warm."
David, 44, Tennessee

David got his safe sex and warm back, and, since his expectations did not include the need for love from stepchildren, he was not disappointed.

Those stepparents in our survey who did not expect immediate love and bonding met with fewer disappointments. "Instant love," especially with older children, is not a realistic goal.

Myth #3: *Having a "New" Mom or Dad Will Be Good For the Children*

One-third of the divorced or widowed adults who participated in our study stated that a very important reason why they had remarried was that they thought it would be "good for the children." This belief can be harmful. Many children don't want a new mother or new father. After the marriage, they may quickly make this clear:

"I hate you! You're not my 'real' mother."

"You can't tell me what to do. You're not my dad."

"I wish you'd die. Then my *real* parents could get back together."

Sticks and stones can break your bones, but words can make your soul bleed. Children act out their emotions, and if they don't want this new package, parents and stepparents end up being the ones who pay the price.

In most cases, it's *the adults* who feel that a two parent family, another "parent" in the home, is important. A third of our survey respondents had consciously searched for a "mother" or "father" for their children. This was a significant factor in their decision to remarry.

"I thought that we'd be one happy family. I wanted my husband to be like a real father to my daughter."

Sandra, 43, South Carolina

"Those kids needed a mother. God knows their real mother never did anything for them."

Robert, 37, Arizona

"I hoped that my daughter would see a good male role model to help her when she would choose a husband.

Peggy, 43, Tennessee

A small number of the participants in our study married *primarily* for the sake of the children. Love and emotional intimacy with the marriage partner were not considered nearly as important as the child-related reasons for remarriage. These men and women reported a significantly *lower* success rate for their marriages than those who married for other reasons.

While parents can get caught up in wanting to provide a new mother or father for their children, prospective stepparents can get emotionally involved in wanting to *be* that mother or father. Emily met and married a widower, Barry, who was raising his children alone. Initially, Emily looked forward to the happy changes she could make.

"I hoped to be a mother to them. I wanted to restore love and happiness to a home that had suffered great loss."

Emily's dream proved unrealistic.

"After the wedding, it was a living nightmare. I loved the children very much and wanted so much to give them a good home. They would have accepted me, but my husband and his family refused to accept us as a family and kept their dead mother alive and were critical of me, turning them against me."
Emily, 38, South Dakota

Roberta experienced a similar situation when she married Bruce who was raising his children alone because of a custody agreement.

"I faced it with missionary zeal. My husband had custody. I would 'save' motherless kids. I believed I was super-parent."

Roberta was soon disappointed.

"It was the hardest and least rewarding work I've ever done."
Roberta, 49, California

Crystal, too, wanted to be a "mother" to her stepchildren.

"I thought I'd be an "instant Mom." This was a very unrealistic expectation which led to problems. I shouldn't have tried to replace their mother."
Crystal, 45, Idaho

Though the majority of our respondents who saw themselves in "rescuer" roles were women, men also overestimated the changes they could make in their new families. When Steve married and began living with his new wife and her son, he looked forward to making a positive impact on his stepson's life.

"I wanted a father/son relationship to develop. I thought I would be able to offer a better role model to the child than his biological father."

This proved impossible.

"My stepson is a hateful, spiteful, ungrateful, argumentative, manipulating, posturing, insecure little creep who refuses to let anyone get close to him. This is very frustrating to me."

Steve, 35, Florida

Just as we cannot create "instant love," neither can we create someone else's happiness nor rescue them from their past. Attempting to do so will frequently cause problems and personal distress for them—*and for us!* The desire to rescue our stepchildren carries with it no guarantee that they *want* to be rescued. We can't be their "Moms" or their "Dads" unless they want us to be.

Myth #4: *Happy Courtships Are Dress Rehearsals for Happy Marriages*

When we asked our respondents to describe the first days of their courtship, they described an idyllic world. The flowers were brighter, the wine tasted sweeter, and, for some, the bedsheets practically caught fire.

Psychopharmacologists tell us that, during the early stages of a romantic relationship, these feelings are quite literally true. Endorphins and enkephalins are produced and released by the brain in significantly greater quantities than normal. The lovers have natural narcotics filling their bodies, giving them more energy, faster pulses, and heightened perceptions.[4] They're on an almost mystical "high." Life is transformed. It's beautiful and wonderful!

Meeting and getting to know the lover's children often become part of the "high." The opportunity to create an instant family can in itself be a romantic image. There are happy picnics, kite flying on Sunday afternoons, pizza and ice cream. Rose colored glasses? Probably. If the first meeting with the children is positive, visions of a loving, happy stepfamily are further reinforced.

Many stepparents-to-be believe that a great first meeting with the prospective stepchildren is a guarantee of good family relationships in the future. The man and the woman love each other, and the children are part of the package. The unveiling of the progeny is an important moment, a critical moment. It *has* to work!

This need is so important to many stepparents that events are often orchestrated to *ensure* that the first meeting is a happy, "perfect" experience.

We spent Christmas together—with dinner, presents, homemade ice cream making, and sledding."
Cheryl, 37, South Dakota

"We all went to Disney World and had a great time!"
Samantha, 26, Texas

"It was our fourth date. We took the girls to a ballet and then walked home where we all played games together."
Karen, 39, New York

"We went roller skating and took all five of the kids with us."

Carla, 41, Michigan

"We went kite flying on a Sunday afternoon."

Ellen, 24, California

Sometimes the first meetings were almost *more* of a success than anticipated. A few of the men and women in our survey became instantly drawn to the children who would later become their stepchildren.

"She was six. He brought her to my house to see me. She just sort of took to me right away. I really wanted children, but I felt, at 42, that it was kind of late to start having them myself. I thought I was always going to be childless, and here was this beautiful little girl—just adorable. I kind of went overboard."

Barbara, 42, Florida

"We met at their house and went to the theatre. She was adorable—quite irresistible. My husband told me that he [had] held off introducing us until our romance was securely underway. He didn't want me to fall in love with this cute, adorable, little girl. He wanted *us* to fall in love first."

Sarah, 34, New York

"The youngest one just crawled into my lap and called me 'Mommy.' I said, 'That's it.' I guess I just knew I'd wind up being 'Mommy,' and I did."

Joyce, 30, Maryland

The desire for a happy blended family is easy to understand. You're in love with a certain woman. That woman has children.

You want to marry a certain man. That man has children. They come as a "package", and you want everything to go right. "I love you very much so *of course* I will love your children—and they will love me!"

Though positive first meetings with the children may be important to you, these first impressions can be deceiving. Sixty-three percent of our survey respondents reported that their first meetings with the children were positive. Yet this fact had *no* statistical correlation with later stepfamily success rates. After the wedding ceremony ends, "real life" begins.

Myth #5: *Bad First Meetings With the Children Guarantee a Bad Marriage*

Tony, one of our respondents, wrote, "Our first meeting as a family was a disaster. I didn't think our marriage stood a chance." Tony decided to marry anyway, and the marriage turned out to be happy and successful.

As with positive first meetings, a bad first experience normally has no impact on future relationships between you, your partner, your children, or your stepchildren. Sometimes, it can be *more* helpful to get a taste of reality without blinders—to see the children in a less than perfect light—right from the start.

Many of our respondents did experience negative first meetings. Bad feelings and tension crept in immediately.

"I babysat for them at their home, and they misbehaved terribly. The oldest one kicked me, and I was flabbergasted that children could be so wild."

Lois, 33, Texas

"The child was four at the time and didn't like seeing "Daddy" holding another woman's hand. She seemed jealous."

Cynthia, 28, New Jersey

"We brought all of our children (six of them) together in my spouse's new "single" apartment for a "family" dinner. Disaster!"

Linda, 47, Washington

"It was horrible! They didn't want to be alone with me."

Wendy, 24, Texas

"We picked the two girls up and took them out for pizza. The oldest, then six, told me her dad planned to marry her mother again very soon."

Marcia, 33, Nebraska

In two percent of first meetings between stepchildren and stepparents, the event was so painful that it seemed the hurt could never be resolved.

"My stepdaughter called for a lunch appointment. She insisted that it be neutral ground and refused an invitation to our house. She revealed the purpose of the meeting at lunch—to visit a lawyer and arrange her father's will."

Vera, 67, Michigan

In a few of our survey responses, stepchildren and stepparents had not met at all, even though the marriage had, in some cases, existed for several years. The stepchildren simply refused to be on the same turf as the stepmother or stepfather.

"I doubt that there will ever be a meeting. The first time I meet them may be at my husband's funeral. They're very angry at him still. They refuse to come to our house even if I'm out of town. We have a child who is their half-brother and they've never even met him. My husband's tried to invite them over if I'm gone, but they've totally refused to do even that. How can we force them?"

Katherine, 32, Texas

Overall, nine percent of our respondents had strongly negative first meetings with the children. Yet, painful though their experiences may have been, these couples did get an early taste of reality, and the success rate for their marriages was almost exactly the same as the rate for families with positive first meetings. Negative first impressions do *not* spell disaster.

Myth #6: *Romantic Love Conquers All*

We asked our participating parents and stepparents to tell us what factors had played a part in their decisions to remarry so that we could evaluate how decisions for second marriages differ from those involved in first marriages. Surprisingly, we found that decisions to marry a second time were made on the same basis as decisions to marry a first time. The involvement of children had little impact on these decisions.

Stepparent Survey
Reasons for Remarriage

Love	89%
Emotional intimacy	87%
Need for companionship	75%
Need for regular sex partner	39%
Family for children	37%
Parent for children	31%
Financial security	29%
Advantages for children	27%
Increased status	12%
Community acceptance	10%

Almost 90 percent of our respondents stated that "love" and "emotional intimacy" had been *very* important in their decision to remarry. These are the identical reasons given by men and women who marry for the first time.

After a failed marriage, the need for romantic love is often so intense that dramatic stories evolve. Larry, a 35 year old California man, placed an ad in the "personals" section of a national newspaper. Twenty-seven year old Paula of Arizona read it and responded. Larry got many responses, but "something special" developed between Paula and himself: they fell in love through their letters. Larry drove to Arizona to meet her in person, and they married that same day. Paula said it was just "a gut instinct." Larry had brought along pictures of his five children, but Paula didn't meet them until she, Larry, and her three children moved to California three weeks later.

At that point, Larry, Paula, and six of the children began living in a two bedroom apartment in California. Larry's other two girls visited for the summer. There were three sets of bunk beds in one room, and the two girls slept on a couch. The love letters were beautiful and romantic, but day-to-day living with eight children was not. Larry and Paula have since separated.

Love *is* very important in any marriage, but, in itself, love is not enough. When two-thirds of those men and women divorcing a second or third time claim that the marriage broke up because of problems related to children, the role of the children in the new marriage *must* be considered, and it's best to do this before the marriage takes place.

If you are planning to remarry, it is highly important to devote advance thought to the role that the children will play in the new marriage. You or your spouse (or both of you) are going to have to work your way into a closed "in-group." Single parents have already developed close ties and bonds with their children. They have a shared history. As you look at their photo albums, you realize a family system already exists. Their relationship predates yours. When you join the family, many adjustments are going to have to be made. It will take more than carefully orchestrated family outings to let you know if you are all going to be compatible.

This does not mean that you are going to have to woo the kids, too. Courting your "new" children is not the answer. Understanding them is. In a second marriage, unlike a first, you and your spouse won't be wrapped in a private cocoon for a few comfortable years prior to the arrival of children. The children are already there.

Start with your love for your spouse (a good relationship between husband and wife is the most important factor in holding a stepfamily together) but also recognize that the children *will* strongly impact your new marriage.

Myth #7: *We'll Be A "Normal" Happy Family Now*

Probably the most destructive myth of all is the expectation that a blended family will quickly become a normal, happy family. This illusion is, in some ways, a culmination of all the others.

Stepparents in our survey were asked: What were your main expectations for your new family? Images of popular television shows and "happily-ever-after" stories from books, movies, and magazines echoed through the replies. Julie Andrews created a happy stepfamily in a few short weeks in *The Sound of Music*. Lucille Ball and Henry Fonda had little trouble handling eighteen kids in *Yours, Mine and Ours*. Many people get caught up in the idealized family lives portrayed on movie and television screens. Watching these families, it all seems easy. All of life's problems are solved in two hours or less.

"I expected us to be one big happy family—the proverbial 'Brady Bunch'."

Marlene, 35, Minnesota

"I wanted us to be the 'Ozzie and Harriet' of stepfamilies. Was that just a dream?"

Paige, 34, Michigan

"We thought we'd have a normal family life."

Katherine, 30, Texas

"What did I expect? To have a happy, secure *normal* family."

Kelli, 26, Pennsylvania

Words that appeared again and again in our survey responses were: "a *normal* family" and "a *happy* family." Kelli even underlined the word "normal" in her answer.

When we remarry, we fantasize about the life we envision for our new family. We want to believe that the old "broken" family is now fixed, that we will be a "real" family again. These fantasies are not only optimistic but illusionistic. We have a vision of what a stepfamily *should* be like. In some ways, we marry a fantasy in addition to a real man or woman with children.

Beliefs about families and what they should be are integral to our emotional make-up. We carry around with us mental images which we focus on our new family. Often these internal pictures are not consciously defined or expressed, but they do carry intense power. As we approach marriage, highly personal scenarios of home and family keep replaying in our hearts and minds.

The reality is that while blended families can eventually be fulfilling, happy, and loving, they truly are very different. Instant shock is more common than instant love. A remarriage is not like a Monopoly game: return to "Go," roll the dice, and hope for better luck the second time around. A second marriage, when children are involved, is more like a kaleidoscope where a turn of the wheel has randomly rearranged all of the pieces. There will be a lot of shifting, a lot of experimenting with different patterns, before it all feels "right," before it feels even close to "normal." Even then, with all the different relationships, all the different reactions and interactions, the end result will be different from our traditional images of home and family.

Yet men and women do avidly seek "normal" families, and it's hard for them to accept that their new family does not fit into the traditional mold. Many people look for a repeat performance of their first marriage; they just want it *to be better* this time around.

Ted was married for thirteen years. His wife left because "she wanted to be a free woman." She agreed to give Ted custody, and soon after the divorce he explained to the children that:

"The space vacated by your mother will someday be filled by someone very special who will love you as much as possible. We will be a normal family again—mother, father, kids, dogs, cats."

Ted did later remarry, but he discovered that just having "someone very special" did not make things "normal" in the sense that he had expected. Life became incredibly difficult for him and for his new wife.

"Being a stepparent is a no-win situation. It is impossible to have a natural family atmosphere. I am not in control of my life or this marriage."

Ted, 44, Florida

There are no guarantees of marital happiness. After the wedding is over and families begin to discover the realities of daily living, they must also begin to realize that they are living in a new kind of family. A new script, new rules, new roles.

HOW DO YOU BEGIN?

On television, blending seems easy—too easy. But "The Brady Bunch" is not reality. The only way that you can truly know in advance what "real life" might be like is to get to know your partner better. The problems that lead to bitter separations are usually present right from the start. How can you assess how strong your marriage will be? Is *your* new blended family likely to endure?

On the following pages are 20 questions for you to answer and 20 matching questions for your partner. Fill in those answers which apply to your situation and then follow the instructions on the page following the questions for an analysis of what your answers reveal.

TWENTY QUESTIONS TO ASK BEFORE REMARRIAGE

"Her" Quiz

1. The most important things I expect from the children are:

_____

_____

_____

2. a. My children should be disciplined by (me/my partner/both):

_____

   b. My partner's children should be disciplined by (me/my partner/both):

_____

3. My preferred methods of disciplining children are:

_____

_____

_____

4. If a serious conflict arises between a stepchild and me, I want my partner to:

_____

_____

_____

5. I feel that the children should participate in the following household chores:

_____

_____

_____

6. If current child custody arrangements change:
   a. My feelings would be:

_____

_____

b. My actions would be:

_____

_____

7. What I most admire about the way my partner handles children is:

_____

_____

8. When my partner has contact with his/her ex-wife/husband/ lover, I feel:

_____

_____

9. When my stepchildren talk about me to their mother/father, I feel:

_____

_____

10. My role in providing for the financial needs of the family will be:

_____

_____

_____

11. My partner's role in providing for the financial needs of the family will be:

_____

_____

_____

12. My participation in household tasks/chores will be:

_____

_____

13. My partner's participation in household tasks/chores will be:

_____

_____

14. After marriage, the social activities we will participate in without the children are:

_____

_____

15. After marriage, the social activities I want the children included in are:

_____

_____

16. My ideal vacation would be:

_____

_____

17. The holiday traditions that are most important to me are:

_____

_____

18. I feel that it is important that the children be present and participate in the following family events or holidays:

_____

_____

_____

19. After we marry, the most important thing I can do for my partner is:

_____

_____

20. After we marry, the most important thing my partner can do for me is:

_____

_____

_____

TWENTY QUESTIONS TO ASK BEFORE REMARRIAGE

"His" Quiz

1. The most important things I expect from the children are:

   _____

   _____

   _____

2. a. My children should be disciplined by (me/my partner/both):

   _____

   b. My partner's children should be disciplined by
      (me/my partner/both):

   _____

3. My preferred methods of disciplining children are:

   _____

   _____

   _____

4. If a serious conflict arises between a stepchild and me,
   I want my partner to:

   _____

   _____

   _____

5. I feel that the children should participate in the following
   household chores:

   _____

   _____

   _____

6. If current child custody arrangements change:
   a. My feelings would be:

   _____

   _____

b. My actions would be:

_____

_____

7. What I most admire about the way my partner handles children is:

_____

_____

8. When my partner has contact with his/her ex-wife/husband/
   lover, I feel:

_____

_____

9. When my stepchildren talk about me to their mother/father,
   I feel:

_____

_____

10. My role in providing for the financial needs of the family will be:

_____

_____

_____

11. My partner's role in providing for the financial needs of the family
    will be:

_____

_____

_____

12. My participation in household tasks/chores will be:

_____

_____

13. My partner's participation in household tasks/chores will be:

_____

_____

14. After marriage, the social activities we will participate in
    without the children are:

_____

_____

15. After marriage, the social activities I want the children included in are:

_____

_____

16. My ideal vacation would be:

_____

_____

17. The holiday traditions that are most important to me are:

_____

_____

18. I feel that it is important that the children be present and participate in the following family events or holidays:

_____

_____

_____

19. After we marry, the most important thing I can do for my partner is:

_____

_____

20. After we marry, the most important thing my partner can do for me is:

_____

_____

_____

To "score" your quiz, give yourself 5 points for each answer that is close in meaning to the answer your partner gave. Add 3 points for each answer which, while not close in meaning, is still acceptable to you. (Note: A few of the questions assume that both of you have children. Add 4 points for each question which does not apply to your family situation.)

Scoring Chart

80 to 100 — You and your partner know each other well. This is a good sign for your stepfamily's future.

65 to 79 — You and your partner are on the right track. You do have a few things to resolve before you happily "blend."

50 to 64 — You and your partner need to talk seriously and resolve your individual needs and expectations.

below 50 — Definite problems lie ahead for your life together. Discuss the issues. Explain your needs. Share your feelings!

A score below 50 usually indicates that you and your partner are going to have to work harder on resolving the differences in your expectations. The time to begin exploring and dealing with your problems is *before* the marriage. Resolving conflicts now will clarify your thinking and give your marriage a happy beginning.

2

Happy Beginnings

When most of us remarry, we aren't twenty-one anymore. We have pasts. We have memories of marriages that ended. We have ghosts and shadows of the pain that living and loving can bring. We hope for that elusive "happily-ever-after," but, at the same time, we're apprehensive as we face the endless plans that have to be made. Many of us have a feeling of *deja vu*. We have walked down this aisle before. While this is another chance, a chance to make everything work out right, it's hard not to wonder: "Will it really be different this time?"

For many remarried couples it *is* different. Their blended family life is better, happier, and more fulfilling than they ever dreamed. For others, the new marriage is as bad—or even worse—than the first one. What makes the difference? Why do some families blend so successfully while others grow more and more discouraged? How can we predict if our blended family will be among the happy ones?

Almost all of the parents and stepparents in our survey experienced some problems after marriage, but many of them were able to work through their difficulties and create strong, healthy families. Achieving this was more than sheer luck. These successful couples handled a number of situations differently—both before and after their remarriage—than couples who were not successful.

There are three areas of premarital preparation that have a direct correlation with subsequent marital happiness and blended family success. They are:

1. Making decisions about the wedding ceremony and honeymoon
2. Planning the new living arrangements
3. Helping the children to adjust emotionally

If more of us took the time to effectively deal with each of these areas *prior* to remarriage, we would have an easier time later. Premarital preparation is an immunization against divorce. None of us can ever be one hundred percent certain that our new marriage will last, but we can do everything possible to give ourselves a happy beginning.

While first marriages which dissolve are most likely to break up *after* five years, second and third marriages end very quickly—more than half *within* the first five years. This is why beginnings are so crucial for men and women who blend families.

PREPARING THE BLUEPRINTS

Should we elope or should we have a formal wedding? If we do decide to have a formal wedding, how formal should it be? Who should be invited? Should our children attend? Should they participate in the ceremony?

In searching for answers to these questions, we begin to lay the groundwork for successfully blending two families. Realistic expectations are very significant, but concrete planning, careful preparation, is even more important. When we remarry, we are building a family, and we need to plan our new life—from the foundation up!

We're All Marrying Each Other!

Dear Mary Ann, Jim and Earl:

We want to help you with your research.

On August 30, 1963, Bud and I got married. We had two brides-maids—our four and five year old daughters—and two best men—our three and six year old sons. The minister later told us that ours was the most beautiful ceremony he had ever performed. That was only the beginning.

For years after that special day, our children told people that we all married each other. They really believed it. When we gathered up our children to take them to their new home, we all felt in our hearts that we were a real family. We eliminated the word "step" from our vocabulary.

We have had 25 years of family life that set good examples for other stepfamilies in our area. At least that is what we were told. We all loved each other and needed each other. Since our wedding day when our children stood up with us at the special ceremony, we have not thought in terms of "step" anything.

Sincerely,

Joanna

Today Bud and Joanna's "bridesmaids" are 29 and 30, and the "best men" are 28 and 31. The family is still a close one. Traditions are important in the family, and they still speak of that August day when they "all married each other." Not long ago, on their twenty-fifth wedding anniversary, they went through a second ceremony—a reaffirmation of their wedding vows:

"All four children stood up with us again. They all marched down the aisle together, and in front of all the witnesses and our friends, the minister read the vows to us, and we repeated them all again."

Joanna, 48, Virginia

The Wedding Ceremony

Second weddings are a bit like childbirth. They're painful. They're joyful. They're filled with hope and new beginnings. At the same time, they contain the seeds of the past at their core. Because of this, many people choose not to have a formal wedding ceremony for a second marriage. They went through the ceremony the first time, and they feel that it's enough now to marry privately in the personal ways that really matter to them. In some situations, this may be the right choice.

For most men and women who remarry, however, a wedding is important and symbolic. While the ceremony stands for romantic love, it is also a celebration of survival. In a world where we have grown accustomed to living apart, our wedding is a symbol of our desire to sanctify our new family, our hope that we can still hold hands together as we face life's challenges. We want "our moment" to be wonderful. Most of all, we want to publicly show our friends and family that there is a rose that grows beneath the winter snows.

First marriages are surrounded by customs and tradition—something old, something new, something borrowed, something blue. White lace and Lohengrin, flower girls and a silk garter for good luck.

Until recently, second marriages have not had these traditions to fall back on. There has been an absence of models. There have also been lingering negative feelings about what is proper and what is not. In the 90's, this is finally changing.

Since blended families have become a major part of the American wedding scene, special ceremonies and new traditions are being created. Daughters are bridesmaids. Sons are best men. Younger children are flower girls and ringbearers. Families often repeat their wedding vows together. Children join their parents in pledging to do their best to make the new family work. Parents promise to help with each other's child-raising responsibilities. Sometimes the children receive their *own* rings. Candles are frequently lit to symbolize the unity and joining of the new family. Ministers often rewrite the vows to announce: "I now unite you as a *family*."

Converting the nuptials from "your" wedding to "our" wedding in the minds of the children can be a tremendous help in gaining acceptance for the new stepparent. A large number of our respondents reported that they had directly involved the children either in the wedding preparations or in the ceremony itself. All of these parents proudly and lovingly related their memories of their "family" wedding.

"Five year old Kathy was my flower girl. She picked out her own dress."

Helene, 31, California

"They were very, very much involved with wedding plans. The kids helped with everything from picking colors to picking up papers at the courthouse. My stepdaughter even helped her dad pick my ring out."

Jerri, 27, Kansas

"I included them in the wedding plans. They all seemed to enjoy it so much—the idea sessions, the shopping, the honor parties."

Linda, 47, Washington

As this "family wedding" tradition grows, even Miss Manners gives her blessing:

"Weddings between people who are well acquainted not only with life, but with each other, should be fascinating occasions. . . . The close relatives whose cooperation adult bridal couples most need are their children. If anyone is to be given a role in the ceremony it should be they. . . . The most destructive etiquette rule there ever was barred children from their parents' subsequent weddings.

". . . Such a wedding is, after all, the beginning of a new life for them, as well as for the bride and bridegroom."[1]

When you find someone with whom you want to spend the rest of your life, you're making one of the most important decisions you will ever make. Is there an "ideal" way to plan your wedding, to take this first step? Much depends on the children, the needs of the couple, and the unique circumstances that surround your family situation.

Don't be overly concerned by old taboos. What about a bachelor party and a groom's cake? What about tossing the wedding bouquet and garter? How do you feel about the entire new family walking down the aisle together? If it feels right to you, make it a part of your wedding ceremony. Some of our respondents even invited ex-husbands and ex-wives to their weddings. Most of us would prefer not to go quite that far, but a decision either way is the *best* way if you feel comfortable with it.

A Wedding Ceremony Quiz

The marriage ceremony is a symbol that, in many ways, will set the tone for your marriage and for your new family's life together. If you choose to have a formal ceremony, you will want it to reflect your needs and style as a couple. Think about your ceremony and what it stands for to you—and to your children! Visualize your ideal wedding and choose the answers in the following quiz that seem appropriate to you. Then ask your fiance/fiancee to take the quiz also—without looking at your responses.

Our Wedding Ceremony

His Answers	Her Answers	**A Couple's Quiz** (Check one or more answers for each of the following questions:)
– – –	– – –	1. Our wedding ceremony will be: a. an "elopement" b. small and intimate c. large with all our friends and family
– – – –	– – – –	2. I believe that our children: a. should not be involved in our wedding b. should attend our wedding ceremony c. should participate in the wedding planning d. should be in the wedding party
– – – –	– – – –	3. I feel that we should: a. use the traditional vows b. write our own vows c. write special vows covering our situation d. include vows for the children to speak
– – –	– – –	4. Our ceremony should be in: a. a church b. a home setting c. some other place _____
– – –	– – –	5. In our ceremony, we want to: a. ignore most traditions b. include many "first marriage traditions" c. establish that our marriage is different by: _____ _____
– – – –	– – – –	6. The bride will walk down the aisle with: (check one) a. her father b. one or more of the children c. her fiance d. no one
– – –	– – –	7. The wedding attire will be: (check one) a. formal b. semi-formal c. informal

After you and your partner have answered the questions, compare your answers. Give yourself 2 points for each matching checkmark. Subtract 1 point for each non-matching mark. Check your score against the table below.

Scoring Chart

10 and above — You're off to a splendid start. Talk about those remaining questions that you disagree on.

5 to 9 — You have some differences. Sit down right now and resolve them.

1 to 4 — Are you sure that you and your partner are talking about the same wedding here? Your ideas are poles apart.

0 and below — Are you sure that it was *your* partner who took the quiz with you? Your wedding could become a war zone!

If there are serious conflicts between the two of you about the ceremony itself, your marriage will begin on a note that's a bit out of tune, and sour notes at this point in the couple relationship can be a prelude to a cacophony of dissonance in your family future together.

You *can* plan a ceremony that both reflects your individual life styles and personalities yet still unites you as one. This is the symbolic beginning of a new life that you will share together. It is important that you plan well, that you create a memory that you will all cherish forever.

The Honeymoon

When Linda and Tom became engaged seven years ago, Linda had three children from a previous marriage, and Tom had two. When Tom picked out Linda's diamond ring, his daughters and stepdaughter went along to help him make a decision. They each got tiny rings to celebrate the occasion. Linda and Tom's wedding ceremony was as idyllic as a Norman Rockwell painting. The five children, beautifully dressed in formals and tuxedoes, were the only attendants at what they referred to as "our parents' wedding." Afterwards, everyone went on a "family honeymoon" to Disney World. A new photo album was started, and dozens of smiling pictures showed scenes of "our wedding" and "our honeymoon."

When Steven and Jacqueline got married five years ago, they recoiled in horror at the thought of a family honeymoon. They chose, instead, to honeymoon in a romantic bridal suite in the Caribbean—alone! They described it poetically: "two pairs of footprints in the sand, a turquoise ocean drenched in white moonlight, a honeymoon nest with a bubbling jacuzzi, fresh flowers, and chilled champagne." Jacqueline surprised Steven with seductive lingerie and his favorite perfume. This couple had wanted time to be together *without their children,* time to focus on themselves and their new relationship. They were at an intensely romantic point in their new marriage, and they wanted to be alone together—sexually and emotionally.

These two families had different answers to the "honeymoon with children" question but equally positive results. Is there a "right" way to handle it? Should you take the kids along on your honeymoon? Many of our respondents did. Many of them also had nightmarish honeymoons.

Although the exact nature of your honeymoon will probably not make or break your marriage, there *was* a strong correlation in our survey between eventual success as a stepfamily and the amount of time a husband and wife spend alone together—without the children. Stepparents who make sure that they have private time to nurture each other feel nourished themselves, and, as a result, view their stepchildren in a more positive light.

Your honeymoon is a very special time for the two of you. It will be over far too soon. We recommend: Leave the children at home!

LAYING THE FOUNDATION

Just as decisions about wedding ceremonies and honeymoons can influence the quality of your new family's life together, so, too, can various other practical considerations. One decision that frequently leads to later problems in blended families is the decision concerning where the new family is going to live. In our survey, 57% of all respondents reported that they lived in either the man or woman's former home after the wedding ceremony while 43% began the marriage living in a new home.

Each of these decisions has advantages and disadvantages.

A New Home, A New Beginning

A new home is symbolic of a new beginning for everyone. Yet it also carries with it requirements for additional adjustments and adaptations during an already emotionally charged time. Our respondents' experiences were mixed.

"We made a plan and enjoyed shopping for a new house for all of us."
Lureen, 38, Oklahoma

"It was hard for the children to adjust to a new neighborhood and new schools in addition to a new parent and new brothers and sisters."
George, 47, Wisconsin

"The children helped in choosing a new home. It was an adventure, and they loved it."

Kathy, 33, Montana

Overall, those respondents who continued to live in their former homes after remarriage were 24% more likely to be *unsuccessful* than those who moved.

When the new family lived in the former home of one of the spouses, the members of the family who had not lived there before often felt like intruders. In addition, the family members who had previously lived in the home frequently felt as if their space had been violated. As a result, most families would have preferred to have moved to a new home. Unfortunately, cost was often the deciding factor in resolving the question of where to live. Many families tried to work around the problem.

"We wanted to get a new home, but real estate activity in Houston hit an all-time low and the old house didn't sell. Instead, we remodeled and made sure each of the children had his or her own room. It wasn't ideal—there were still 'space wars'—but it seemed our only option at the time."

Ann, 45, Texas

"We couldn't afford to move, but we did let all the children decorate their own rooms. This made it seem more like their own territory."

Al, 44, Texas

In some situations, when things didn't work out, the home itself became a symbol of the festering problems in the relationship.

"They moved into my home because I didn't want to live in a home that he'd shared with his wife. We just handled it all wrong. It was disastrous. They think of the house as *my* house. My kid kind of got left out in the cold. Because his kids had to adjust, we concentrated on them, and now mine is the one who has suffered; he's the one we've had problems with."

Carolyn, 35, Utah

One couple in our survey actually separated for eleven months because a husband did not keep his promise to move the new family to another home.

"After living in my spouse's former house for three and one-half years, I moved out to an apartment with my son for eleven months. When I moved back to the house, it was with the understanding we would sell and build a home of our own."

Carol Anne, 45, Texas

For Carol Anne and Roger, the new home was the only way to avoid a divorce.

Decorating: "His and Her" Furniture

In addition to questions about where to live, many other practical considerations revolving around the new family's living arrangements come into play. In a second marriage, the cherished possessions of two households also must "blend." Houston's Jane Page of Jane Page Creative Designs has worked with a number of blended families in the sensitive area of blending furnishings and possessions to create a home environment where everyone feels comfortable. Page notes that since "his and her" furniture can provide some touchy times, you may "need to call in an objective third party who's not sentimentally attached to this or that, someone who can make decisions based on good design. Of course just like in a marriage, you do have to be sensitive to certain wishes and make some compromises."[2]

Not everyone can afford an interior designer to "blend" possessions, but everyone must work together to make decisions regarding the new family's home. If she loves that antique lamp which was a gift from Great Aunt Jennie and he hates it, what will become of it? Should you give it away? Display it prominently? Put it in a back room?

These questions may seem trivial *before* the marriage takes place, but it's often the "little things" that cause the greatest problems *after* the wedding. The more planning that you can do before you begin living together, the greater your chances will be for avoiding serious conflicts later.

The Most Important Consideration: *Preparing the Children*

While it's important that you take the time to discuss the ceremony, the honeymoon, and the post-marriage living arrangements, the most important consideration of all is preparing the children.

We asked our survey respondents: "Did you prepare your children in any way for your remarriage?" Surprisingly, forty percent of all those answering the question said "No."

Many of those who answered "No" stated that marriage was a personal decision involving only the couple themselves. They stressed that they were adults, that they had their own needs, and that they did not feel it necessary to "prepare" others or to have their children "validate" their decisions. A number of parents were adamant in their feelings that it was their own wedding and their own decision.

"We didn't need to ask permission!"
Helene, 48, Massachusetts

Others noted that the ages of their children had been a factor in not discussing the decision.

"My son was only three."
Dottie, 26, Ohio

"My children were in their twenties."
Allen, 58, Texas

"I didn't prepare them. They were pretty well grown. After ten years of widowhood, they had been the ones who thought I should put an ad in the 'Globe' newspaper."
Jeanne, 55, Wyoming

Many parents thought it was better to take "the marriage step" first and let the children get used to it.

"I didn't tell them beforehand—but all eight children liked him."
Jane, 32, Texas

"I'm not sure how they felt about it. We all never talked about it."
Norma, 37, Idaho

Parents without custody, especially, did not feel obligated to tell the children or prepare them beforehand.

"I just announced it. After all, I was not the custodial parent."
Joseph, 62, Illinois

Other parents simply made an announcement which, in some cases, was startlingly businesslike. Discussion was minimal.

"I briefed them on my new husband."
Lucinda, 32, Texas

"I just informed them that we were planning to marry and a stepkid would be moving in with us."
Jill, 39, California

"I told them they would have a new dad and a new brother and they were to treat them as they treated me—with respect, caring, and friendship."
Elaine, 40, Washington

In still other situations, the children lived in other cities or states. This made it especially difficult to discuss the impending marriage at length or in depth.

"We drove to Chicago where my daughter lives so she could meet him before the wedding. My oldest met him for the first time the night before the wedding."
Jean, 48, Iowa

"My son and I flew to Indiana from Arizona to visit him and his kids, and he flew out to get to know my son."
Laura, 40, Indiana

Sixty percent of our respondents *did* prepare their children in one way or another. Most importantly, two-thirds of those respondents *with successful stepfamilies* had prepared their children

dren for the impending marriage. Many of the parents who did not prepare their children beforehand did not realize the impact of the decision that was being made.

When Sheryl, 29, married Daniel, 34, she had never met his four children, ages three through ten. Sheryl had five children of her own, ages three through eleven. Because Sheryl enjoyed her own children so much, she looked forward to the first summer that Daniel's children would visit. She did not feel that his children would pose any problem, so it had not seemed important to meet them.

"I had not even met any of his children until one month after our marriage, but I was very optimistic and flexible. They came from their home in Wyoming to visit us. Somehow, it wasn't 'real life.' We tried to make it real life, but it was a facade. I'm a relaxed person, but when they come to visit, I get really uptight because I have a hard time being myself. My husband feels that I should feel the same way about his kids as he does about mine, but that just can't possibly be. Their mother is raising them differently than I'm raising my children. Sometimes my husband's past makes me want to forfeit the future, and that's sad. Sometimes I wish Wyoming would *blow up* and disappear from the earth.

Sheryl, 33, Utah

Children *do* need to be prepared for remarriage. As many couples discover, planning and participating in a beautiful wedding ceremony can be a strong symbol of family commitment and can provide loving memories to cherish through the years. But the most important reason for advance preparation is the need to *emotionally* prepare the children for the inevitable changes that will occur as the new family begins its life together.

THREE MAJOR FEARS KIDS HAVE ABOUT BLENDED FAMILIES

Most families contemplating remarriage do not seek premarital counseling or attend workshops or even read material on the subject. Less than one percent of our respondents mentioned having sought *any* type of premarital counseling to prepare themselves or their children for stepfamily living. The feelings of optimism surrounding a remarriage tend to obliterate potential questions and doubts on the part of parents. Those same feelings also tend to minimize any recognition of children's fears. Yet most children, whether they verbalize it or not, harbor some very natural fears in the following three areas.

Fear #1: *Will There Be Enough Love?*

One of the biggest fears that children have is: Will there be enough love to go around? Not only is there a new parent on the scene but new brothers and sisters as well. It is extremely important to talk about this concern *before* marriage. Many parents do.

"I tried to explain that we were going to become a family with more people, and things would be different, but I loved them just as much."
Joyce, 39, Iowa

"I talked to the stepchildren a lot. I let them know that their dad's caring for me did not mean they were losing him."
Dawn, 36, Massachusetts

"Father and daughter talked alone to explain why we were going to marry and that Daddy still loves her very much."

Cynthia, 28, New Jersey

Knowing that Daddy or Mom still "loves you very much" can be extremely reassuring to a child.

Fear #2:
Will These Changes Cause Problems for Me?

When preparing children for blended family living, parents should be realistic. While there will be positive changes, there will also be adjustments.

One innovative family with young children turned their discussion of the "pros" and "cons" of stepfamily life into a game. Twenty-five cents was given for every advantage and every disadvantage that could be named. Some of the children's responses were quite realistic; others, merely wishful.

Advantage:
"Mom will be too tired to cook so we'll go out for pizza a lot."

Tammy, 10

Disadvantage:
"What if I have to go to the bathroom and someone's already in both of them?"

Andy, 6

Other respondents used a more formal approach in talking with their children about advantages and disadvantages.

"I told them that we would be getting married and his son would be living with us and that there would be some changes but that I hoped we would be able to handle them."

Sally, 37, Pennsylvania

"I asked him how he liked Don and what would he think if I decided to remarry. I asked him what he didn't like, too."

Carolyn, 37, Texas

"We talked about the things that would change—some good and some not so good. We stressed the importance of being flexible."

Sandy, 38, Virginia

Helping children "come to grips" with what to expect—the positives and the negatives—results in their feeling less apprehensive about the significant changes which *are* taking place in their lives.

Fear #3:
What Control Do I Have?

Since children fear the feeling of having no control over their own lives, they should be allowed *some* input into their parent's upcoming marriage. It's so easy for them to feel left out at this very important time. They usually love to be included in wedding preparations and in planning the new living arrangements. Helping select flowers, food, and clothes for the wedding and choosing colors and decorations for a new bedroom are positive ways in which they can be involved in the process. They'll feel like important members of the team and will realize that this is a special time for them, too. Parents reap later rewards if they help their children feel like participants rather than mere bystanders.

If children are given too much power in the decision making process, however, it can be frightening to them. If, for example, they control a parent's decision to marry, if they are given the final decision on *whether* to marry, they are being granted a power that may cause problems later.

Some of our respondents felt that they could not marry unless their children were in favor of the new arrangement. These parents knew that problems can be created when families merge, and they hoped to avoid them by seeking their children's and stepchildren's "approval."

"I asked their permission to marry."

Marlys, 48, Indiana

"He and his son proposed to me and my sons."

Fran, 43, Virginia

"I told them their opinions were most important. If they could not accept him, there would be no marriage. He knew this, too."

Marjorie, 45, Pennsylvania

Were these parents and stepparents merely being realistic or were they giving their children a power of validation over adult lives? It's often a fine line to walk. While communication with the children about remarriage is essential, we also need to be aware that it can be very frightening to a child to be given a decisional role in a parent's life.

SUCCESSFUL BLENDING

Anything that can be done to resolve potential stepfamily problems before marriage will have a positive impact later. If stepparenting workshops are available in your area, attend them. If there is a local stepparent support group, make arrangements to visit it and listen as others share their feelings and experiences.

Above all, try to prepare the children. Many of our respondents felt, in retrospect, that they should have prepared their children more fully for the new marriage.

"We were too naive to realize that we needed to prepare them."

Melodie, 42, Minnesota

"My husband and I did not discuss these important issues enough. We came to realize this later."

Lisa, 41, Florida

"My children knew of the engagement and wedding plans. My only regret is, we did not have them at the wedding. We feel, even 23 years later, that it was a big mistake!"

Vera, 61, Illinois

When children are involved, *families* get married. The expression "blending" is used more and more, but new families rarely blend perfectly. They bring the past with them: different values, different experiences, different histories. Suddenly the wedding vows are spoken, and everyone is supposed to live happily ever after. Rarely did that happen in fairy tales, and it does not happen in "real life" either.

Webster's definitions of "blending" are:[3]

- to pass gradually or imperceptibly into each other, as colors.
- to go well together; harmonize.
- to mix; merge; unite.

We'll never achieve the first definition—nor would we desire to. Children and adults do not need or want to "pass gradually into each other, as colors." Families *do* want to "go well together." We do want to live in harmony. Husbands and wives do need to "unite."

Rather than trying to be indistinguishable from each other, be grateful for the unique past each person brings into the new family. Strive to "go well together," to "harmonize," to "unite" as a successful blended family.

If you are one of the million men and women going into a blended family this year, make your choices wisely. The patterns that you set *before* the wedding will help you *after* marriage— much more than you can realize right now.

Part Two

After
The Wedding Ball
Is Over

3

The United Front

When we tried to decide how to begin this section of our book, a number of topics competed for first place. We chose the "united front" because it is truly the underlying concept required for successful stepfamily living. Without a "united front," remarried couples are very likely to go through another divorce. With a "united front," the chances are nine out of ten that the new marriage and family will thrive and succeed. As parents in a blended family, we must create a "united front" first—before we deal with any of the specific problems and challenges that come with the blending process. We must, as a couple, "unite," mutually agreeing upon a course of action and firmly standing together as we deal with our children and stepchildren.

WHY A UNITED FRONT?

Being a stepparent is different than being a parent. We can be single and still be mothers and fathers, but we have to be part of a couple relationship to become stepmothers and stepfathers. Stepparenthood is exclusively for men and women living together. This fact alone creates the biggest problem of all for many of us as we begin to blend our families. Without the biological father's direct support, the stepmother has no power over his children. Without the natural mother's endorsement, the stepfather cannot be truly effective as a co-parent. A stepfamily cannot be successful if the couple relationship is not strong and committed.

Stepfamily conflicts call up predictable responses in stepparents. Our attitudes toward our stepchildren are highly dependent on whether or not we and our spouses have a solid understanding. If I, as a stepmother, have a husband who supports me and stands behind me in dealing with his children, I will feel better about my husband, my stepchildren, and myself. I will also be more likely to succeed as a stepmother. On the other hand, if my husband berates the way I handle his children and sides with them in conflicts, I will lose not only power and authority with them but confidence in myself as well. If I am a stepfather and my wife is my ally, I am more apt to be happy in my stepfather role. If, however, she undermines my efforts or openly criticizes me when I interact with her children, I will most likely grow resentful.

Pulling Together

When a family blends, conflict is inevitable. This is simply a fact of life. Conflicts may end in new insights and greater fulfillment, or they may end in a bitterness that will tear the family apart. Few people visualize accurately what lies ahead for them after the wedding is over. As the new stepfamily absorbs new people and begins to make choices, many issues arise. The couples who make it are the ones who find ways to resolve their conflicts. The ones who do not make it are the ones who allow themselves to become overwhelmed by their blending problems.

If you have ever tried to paddle a canoe with another person, you know that you have to coordinate your efforts. If you don't, the canoe will go round and round in circles, never getting anywhere. New stepfamilies often go round in circles, too, unable to move constructively forward, out of control as they try to get on with their lives. They replay certain issues over and over again in an unending circular pattern, never getting to their destination, never even learning to enjoy the trip.

Again and again stepparents in our survey used the term "tug-of-war." Three-quarters of our respondents felt that they had, on occasion, experienced a problem in this area.

"I feel that I'm in the middle—in a tug-of-war. It's either my husband and I or my daughter and I."

Kathy, 40, Massachusetts

"I wanted my husband to be like a real father to my daughter, but this 'family' did not happen. There was divisiveness around the children, and I was in the middle."

Sandra, 43, South Carolina

"I sometimes feel like an intruder in my own home."

Jeanne, 26, Ohio

Frustrations mount. The stepparent feels caught between parent and child. The parent feels caught between stepparent and child. Both adults feel pulled in two directions, caught "in the middle." The scenario is ripe for game playing, for testing. Who can manipulate whom to get what he/she wants? Who loves whom the most? How far will he/she go? Am I second best in this family? *Are the kids more important than I am?*

Love is Not Enough

The first year in a stepfamily is extremely tough. Despite strong initial bonds of love, the majority of couples that do break up have problems right from the start. More than half of those remarriages that break up do so within the first five years.

After five years, the success rate is higher. The couples who last that long have, of necessity, started to come to grips with the pitfalls of blended family living. They have found ways to deal with those inevitable blending conflicts.

In our survey, 94 percent of happy and successful stepfamilies showed a strong ongoing bond between the husband and wife. The relationship of the couple to each other was the key factor in blending success.

In 94% of Remarriages:
A Strong Husband/Wife Bond = Happy, Successful Families

In most cases, couples who achieved this bond did not just "fall into it" when they fell in love; rather, they had to learn specific skills to achieve their unity.

Dr. Andrew Cherlin, author of *Marriage, Divorce, Remarriage,* believes that second marriages have a higher rate of failure than first marriages because there are so few families who know how to successfully blend.[1] Couples are not prepared for the special and unique problems that they will instantly face. No clear-cut blueprints of behavior have yet evolved to help couples instinctively deal with the myriad of challenges that confront them. The moves are clear for first marriages, but, in second marriages, couples often "wing it." Sometimes this works—often it does not. The remarried family and its interrelationships are both incredibly complex and radically different from the relationships involved in a nuclear family.

The message is clear. When we remarry, love alone is never enough. We must understand this in the depths of our souls. If our marriages are going to succeed, love must be more than just a four letter word, more than an emotion, more than a feeling. In a blended family, love must also be a behavior. Translating *feelings* of love into the *actions* of love is the only way to create a marriage and a stepfamily that will last.

Converting Feelings to Actions

Our United Front approach for dealing with blended family problems focuses on actions—not emotions, on deeds—not feelings. Virtually all of our survey respondents had some difficulties as they began the blending process. Yet more than three-fourths of those couples who had happy and successful stepfamilies directly or indirectly used the United Front approach to work through their difficulties and create strong families. The couples who were able to resolve their problems were the men and women who were committed to each other and who "stuck together" as a couple when they dealt with the children.

Remarried couples who stick together stay together! In nuclear families, the children are often the glue that binds the marriage together. First marriage couples often stay together "for the sake of the children." In blended families, the opposite is true; the children are usually the couple's most divisive force. Two-thirds of divorcing stepparents state that children are the cause of their breakup. Staying married "for the sake of the children" rarely happens in a remarriage. Remarried couples stay together only as long as the man and the woman are happy with each other.

When we listen to other people talk about their marriages, we learn much about them. But, at the same time, we also learn much about ourselves. As writers, we found again and again that many of our respondents were mirrors of ourselves. The problems they had, we had, too. The challenges they faced were the same challenges we had faced.

In our own blended family, we did not begin using the United Front approach when we first married. We had a glimmer of the concept and several strong hints of the need for it, but, in reality, the approach finally fell into place as we learned it from our respondents while working on this book.

the approach finally fell into place as we learned it from our respondents while working on this book.

We wish we had understood it fully and been able to use it earlier. A lot of hurt and pain—and many angry confrontations—could have been avoided. Our children would have started their blended family life in a more stable environment. They would not have gone through that period of insecurity when their parents were "caught in the middle," not knowing whether to side with the "unreasonable" child or the "unreasonable" spouse. For us, learning and using United Front techniques have made a great difference in our lives.

Perhaps you already use this approach in your own marriage; maybe you don't. Check your United Front "Quotient" on the following page. This is a quick way to discover whether you and your spouse are using United Front techniques.

Your United Front Quotient

Your United Front Quotient (Circle *one* answer for each question)	Nearly Always	Often	Sometimes	Almost Never
1. Do you and the children keep "secrets" from your spouse?	A	B	C	D
2. If you tell one of the childeren to do something, does your spouse support that order?	D	C	B	A
3. Do your spouse and the children keep "secrets" from you?	A	B	C	D
4. If your spouse gives an order to one of the children, do you support that order?	D	C	B	A
5. When there is a disagreement between a child and a stepparent, does the parent side with the stepparent?	D	C	B	A
6. Do you *or* your spouse make decisions concerning the children without discussing those decisions with each other?	A	B	C	D
7. Do you and your spouse discuss the problems either of you have with the other's children?	D	C	B	A
8. Do you and your spouse resolve, to the satisfaction of *both* of you, the problems you have with the other's children?	D	C	B	A

After completing the self-test, grade yourself as follows: each "D" answer is worth 15 points, each "C" is worth 10, and each "B" is worth 5. "A" answers have a zero value. If your total score is under 100, you and your spouse are not doing everything you can to ensure the success of your stepfamily.

Our survey made two things clear. First of all, stepfamily conflicts are *normal.* This fact cannot be emphasized strongly enough. Secondly, the difference between successful and unsuccessful stepfamilies lies in how those conflicts are handled.

Wishing is Also Not Enough

Before discussing specific United Front techniques, we need to become aware of the counterproductive methods that we are apt to use unthinkingly when we face blending problems.

Newly remarried couples often spend a lot of time wishing.

"I wish my stepson would at least say 'thank you' once in a while!"
Mary, 44, Texas

"I wish I could just do something for myself and not always have to wonder what they want."
Jerri, 30, Texas

"I'm always wishing that things could be different."
Sue, 33, Texas

"I wish that I didn't feel like I'm always on the outside looking in."
Marianne, 41, Illinois

"I wish that his daughter knew how to give. She takes and takes but never gives. At 7, I wouldn't have expected much, but at 18?—come on!"
Denise, 29, Tennessee

"I wish the kids didn't treat me as if I were just a maid."
Ruth, 54, South Dakota

"I wish they would buy *me* something sometime. I buy their birthday and Christmas presents but they never buy me anything—and then they thank their dad for the things I buy them."

Karen, 49, Indiana

"I wish I could be happy again." "I wish someone cared about *me*." "I wish the stepkids would just disappear!"

If wishes were horses, beggars would ride. Wishing, without acting, simply makes things worse. Yet couples who marry for a second (or third) time often go out of their way to avoid any kind of confrontation with each other. Perhaps their last marriages ended with a lot of conflict, and so now they are going to avoid anything that even resembles disagreement. Instead, they repress their unhappiness and anger and try to pretend everything is fine. As a result, they end up internally bombarding themselves with "wish" statements and "what if" questions.

- What if I make her mad and this marriage breaks up, too?
- What if I force my husband to choose, and he sides with his kids over me?
- What if her kids end up hating me?

It isn't enough to merely "wish" or ask "what if." It also isn't enough to just say "I feel angry" or "I can't stand it when *your* son leaves his underwear on the floor." We need to do more than that. We need communication tools, tools that work even under the stress of stepfamily living. Parents in a stepfamily need a structured method of communication to deal with their blending conflicts.

Structured Communication, a method of conflict resolution (and the first of our Strategies for Stepfamily Success), is the key technique which allows remarried couples to build a United Front. It is based on the commitment of the husband and wife to each other and to the success of their blended family. This foundation of caring commitment is essential.

STRUCTURED COMMUNICATION: Seven Steps To Stepfamily Success

A blended family can be extremely rewarding or it can be total chaos. When problems arise—and they will—we often tend to see ourselves as victims. We feel like powerless pawns, caught in this maze of chance, these unpredictable relationships. In reality, we do have some control. Alone, we cannot completely change the situation, but we can start moving the relationships—and the stepfamily—in a more positive direction.

In a given situation, we might reasonably feel that a problem is not "our" problem, that we did not create it. Perhaps we didn't, but, if it bothers us, it is "our" problem. We need to take the initiative for setting a time and place for discussion. This is the first step of the Structured Communication technique.

Step 1: *Set A Time and Place*

In difficult blended family situations, a simple "I wish" or "if only," spoken or unspoken, will not solve the problem. Neither will an expectation that our spouse is going to recognize our distress and quietly "fix" it for us. It may happen, but it may not. If we are feeling uncomfortable about something that has happened in our family, we need to let our partners know that we want to talk privately.

Ask if this is a good time. If it is not, make an appointment at a mutually agreed upon time.

Since *we* are the ones concerned, it is *our* responsibility to initiate this request. It is our partner's responsibility to respond to the request. If at all possible, the appointment should be arranged to take place within twenty-four hours. If problems are "held" for longer than that, they begin to fester and to affect other aspects of our daily lives.

Step 2: *State The Problem*

What *really* happened? We need to come to grips with this sometimes slippery question ourselves and then tell our partners what our problem is.

Define the problem precisely and specifically. What happened? When did it happen? Where did it happen? Who did what? Who said what? Do not get into the "whys." "Whys" tend to be guesses which may or may not be valid. "Whys" tend to be perceived as accusations, and most people do not respond well to accusations when they may already be feeling stressed by the situation. Simply state the facts.

Step 3: *Define Our Needs*

What do we truly want to happen? We probably "want it all," but we need to limit ourselves to the specific problem and situation. We need to: (1) clearly identify to our partners what our needs are—what actions and what results we would like to see, (2) be honest with ourselves in exploring what our *real* needs are, and (3) be very careful not to understate those needs. We should not say that our need is "to have those girls make their beds in the mornings" when our problem is that we are angry because our stepdaughters ignored us when we asked them to make their beds. Our real need in this example is probably that we want our stepdaughters to treat *all* of our reasonable requests with respect.

Be precise and be honest.

Step 4: *Listen To Our Partner's Needs*

When we're angry, listening to our partners objectively is not easy. Some of our residual resentment spills over and lands right on them. At a gut level, our emotions are reminding us that if we hadn't married that man (or woman) we wouldn't have this problem in the first place!

While this may be true, it's not helpful, and if we want our marriage to work, we have to listen to our partners' observations and needs as they reply to our concerns. We might be given exactly what we want. On the other hand, we may not. Acknowledge the stated feelings. We don't have to agree with them, but we must let our partners know that we have heard them, that we understand what is being said. If we don't understand something, we need to explore the point further.

Don't argue about what has been said. Just accept the feelings at this point and try to understand what they are.

Step 5: *Identify Potential Solutions*

After defining our needs and listening to our partners' needs, we get to the most difficult part: asking ourselves some crucial questions. Each of us needs to ask ourselves:

1. What would be my *ideal* solution to this problem?
2. What would be acceptable?
3. What would be unacceptable?
4. How far could I go in compromising?
5. What are my *absolute* boundaries?

No one should have to "lose face" in the solution. Be creative and explore all possible compromises, with the clear goal of resolving the conflict in a way that will allow *both* partners to feel satisfied with the outcome. Try not to get stuck in the negotiation process at this point. There are probably more options than are immediately apparent. Take the time to search for them.

Step 6: *Decide On A Single Solution*

We have to be true to ourselves when we decide on the "best" solution. *Both* partners must feel comfortable with it. We can't give in to something that we can't support, yet we have to be open to some compromise. We must recognize our boundaries and ask ourselves the questions:

1. What can I give up from my ideal solution and what can't I give up?
2. Am I being entirely reasonable about my boundaries?
3. Is my partner?
4. Is the point under discussion really that serious?
5. If not, can we trade off: this point to my partner, the next one to me. "You give on this; I'll concede on that."

If the problem is serious, then both partners must find common ground; a marital relationship is truly at stake. Perhaps it will be necessary to go back and explore potential solutions again, recognizing at the same time how highly important it is that both partners agree on a solution.

Step 7: *Implement Your United Front Solution*

After we have worked out a solution that we both agree on, we absolutely have to support each other fully in front of the children. Under no circumstances should we cave in to their demands or allow them to change our minds on the solution we've agreed upon. Children by their very nature love to "divide and conquer." They often feel powerful when they place parents in a "tug-of-war" situation. Do not give in. Children label as unfair anything which is not exactly what *they* want.

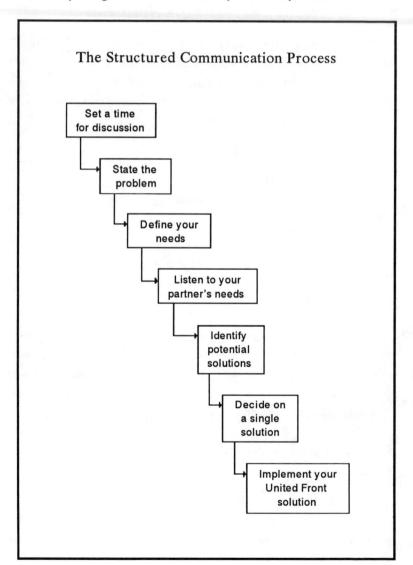

The Structured Communication Process

USING STRUCTURED COMMUNICATION

Let's consider how a hypothetical couple, whose conflict reflects a common blended family situation, used Structured Communication to resolve their problem.

Bill and Karen had a conflict revolving around how to spend New Year's Eve. Bill's children had come to Nebraska from California to spend the holidays. Since they would be going back home on New Year's Day, Bill wanted to celebrate with them on New Year's Eve. Karen and Bill were also asked to a New Year's Eve party which Karen wanted very much to attend. Many of her old school friends were home for a short time for the holidays, and this would probably be her only chance to see them. Bill took the lead in seeking a resolution of the problem.

Step 1: *Set A Time and Place*

Bill: Let's just stop yelling and sit down and talk seriously about this.

Karen: Why? So you can talk me into doing what you want again?

Bill: You're the one who always seems to get what you want. Listen, we're both upset now. Let's talk upstairs at 10 o'clock tonight after the kids are in bed.

Accusations are not productive in solving problems. Someone needs to stop the process and get the discussion headed forward. Bill allowed both himself and Karen a chance to unwind and chose a time when they could talk without interruptions.

Step 2: *State The Problem*

Bill: I want to spend New Year's Eve with the kids. They go back home on New Year's Day, and I won't see them again till summer.

Karen: I don't want to spend New Year's Eve with the kids. I've been a cook and a maid this whole vacation, and now I just have one tiny request—going to the party to see my friends. Don't you care at all about how I feel?

Bill: You sure don't seem to care about how I feel.

Karen: We do have a problem. That's for sure.

Once again, it was difficult not to let emotional feelings intrude in the discussion. It is important to state the facts, what the problem is, not to linger on the "whys."

Step 3: *Define Your Needs*

Bill: Since I won't be seeing the children again till summer, I want to end this visit on a positive note. I want them to have happy memories and want to come back, and I want you to understand how I feel about that.

Karen: And I want you to understand my feelings. I haven't seen some of my friends for over three years. If I have to give up this party for your children, *I'm* certainly not going to have happy memories of their visit. I really need a night off—without kids.

Karen and Bill both had legitimate needs, and they were honest in expressing them. This time they stuck to expressing their own needs, without undermining the needs of their partner.

Step 4: *Listen To Your Partner's Needs*

Bill: It sounds like this party is very important to you. You want to see your friends and you want us to have some time together without kids.

Karen: Exactly. That is important to me. But I also understand how you feel about the kids. Everything has gone pretty good so far, and you want to keep things happy.

Bill: Yeah. I hate bad endings or blow-ups with someone I won't see for awhile.

Karen: I know you do—especially when those "someones" are your kids.

Bill and Karen not only understood the needs of one another, but they provided verbal feedback to let each other know that they did understand. Though their own needs were still important to them, they started to take their partner's needs into consideration.

Step 5: *Identify Potential Solutions*

Bill: What should we do?

Karen: What do *you* want to do?

Bill: I want us to go out for pizza—all of us. Then to a movie. Then home for fireworks. That's how we always spent New Year's in my family.

Karen: In my family, my parents went out on their own, and all of us kids accepted it. We didn't feel that we had to always be included in everything.

Bill: Isn't there anything we could do that would make us both feel good?

Karen: Not if it means I'd have to give up the party.

Bill: Maybe we could do both. We could spend part of the
          evening with the kids and then go to the party later?

Karen: That might work. And you wouldn't be angry?

Bill: Not if we can spend part of the evening with them and
          get the fireworks in.

Karen: Sounds like it could work. What time would we get to
          the party?

*This is a simplified version of a process that probably would
have taken much longer. Usually there are many potential solutions to any problem, and it's important to identify and consider
the best options.*

Step 6: *Decide On A Single Solution*

Bill: Okay, it's agreed then? We'll take the kids out for an
          early movie and pizza, and we'll get home just after
          dark for the fireworks.

Karen: Then we'll leave for the party by 10 o'clock and stay till
          it's over?

Bill: It's a deal.

*Bill and Karen were able to compromise and negotiate, reach-
ing a solution that was acceptable to each of them. In some cases
a solution is reached quickly. In others, the process is long and
arduous. The important thing is that both parties must agree. One
cannot just go halfheartedly along with the decision. If both parties do not agree, then they need to go back and rethink their list
of potential solutions. A solution should not be a "winner/loser"
type of agreement.*

Step 7: *Implement Your United Front Solution*

The hardest part for Bill and Karen was maintaining a United Front when the children protested.

Bill's children: It's not fair! We always do the fireworks at midnight. Mom wouldn't go out and leave us on New Year's Eve.

Bill: I know you're disappointed, but Karen and I have needs, too. Let's all work together to make this a fun night for all of us.

The decision had been made, the United Front agreement was kept, and the children not only did not suffer by it, but they also began to realize that guilt trips and manipulation were not going to work with their father and his new wife. It wasn't that Bill didn't care about them; it was that he did care—cared enough to maintain his parental authority in dealing with them, cared enough to provide a happy and stable home for them during their visits.

DIVORCE INSURANCE

Forming a United Front at the beginning of a remarriage is insurance against divorce. It keeps the marital "couple relationship" strong. It also adds stability to the children's lives as they realize that their parents are in control and cannot be manipulated. Stepfamilies are formed from fragments of other family units. Holding those fragments together can be very difficult. The United Front is the *glue* that keeps the blended family strong and whole.

4

Aftershock

Virtually all stepparents suffer "aftershock" following remarriage. Most of us are embarrassed by it. We feel that we are alone, that we are the only ones asking ourselves:

- What's wrong?
- What happened?
- Why did everything suddenly change?

We find ourselves feeling stunned and shocked. We never expected it to be like this. The main reasons that many of us experience aftershock are that:

1. Our expectations for remarriage were very unrealistic. We fantasized about "The Brady Bunch" and, instead, we ended up with "Real Life."
2. We did not adequately prepare ourselves or our children for the problems and adjustments of living in a blended family.

Before marriage, only one percent of our survey respondents had attended a support group or sought counseling to gain more information about blending. After marriage, this figure soared. Fifty percent of parents and stepparents sought outside help in working through problems. It does not take long to realize that blended family living is not easy!

Aftershock is *normal* for families who blend. As the new family moves from the fantasy phase into the reality phase of step-family living, stepparents must be prepared for the conflicts that will inevitably arise. It's time to begin redefining the family. As Mark Twain once said of the transition from sail to steam on the Mississippi River, "When it's steamboat time, you steam."

Twain's statement is valid, but, as we discovered from our survey, "steaming" is much easier to talk about than to do. One of the most rewarding—and disturbing—parts of writing this book was interviewing parents in blended families across the country. The parents and stepparents in our survey came from many different walks of life. They were construction workers and doctors, lawyers and secretaries, welfare recipients and retirees, homemakers and Broadway actresses, farmers and supermarket cashiers. Their educational levels ranged from 8th grade to M.D.'s and Ph.D.'s. The youngest child in these families was one month old; the oldest was fifty-one. Some families were poor; others were wealthy. All of them were anxious to talk to someone—someone they would only know as a one-time voice on the telephone. Again and again, we heard their stories. The scenarios and characters were different, but the theme was usually the same: life changes *drastically* after the wedding ceremony. Again and again, parents and stepparents said:

- I can't believe what I got into.
- He doesn't even seem like the man I married anymore.
- Her kids were great when we were dating, but now they make my life unbearable.

The realization comes to most remarried couples as a wave of shock and denial: "This can't be happening to us. To me!"

It does happen, and we need to openly confront it and work through it. Chances are our expectations weren't that realistic. We had beautiful projections of what we wanted this marriage and family to be. Many of us married images: images of men or women, images of family life. After marriage, we found ourselves living with "real" people, people who were very different from the images we had pictured in our minds.

Aftershock happens to most of us, and less than half of us survive it. Those of us who do survive have a good chance of creating a happy blended family. Never for a moment, though, should any of us expect our new life to be easy. Remarried life—with children—is difficult, and we need to "come to grips" with that fact early.

PREDICTABLE CONFLICTS WHEN FAMILIES BLEND

Though there are many problems that arise during the first year of marriage, our survey showed that the two most common ones are:

1. How to handle all those "little" annoyances and irritations that seem minor at the time but end up driving us crazy.
2. How to deal with emotional triangles and jealousy that form within the stepfamily structure.

If the family unit does not break up first, these problems will usually resolve themselves within five years. They are a problem primarily at the outset of a marriage, when families actually begin living together and realize, "This isn't casual dating anymore. This is permanent!"

THE "LITTLE THINGS"

A child's failure to say thank you for a gift. A constant "no thank you" at the dinner table. Wet towels on the bathroom floor. These annoyances might seem insignificant. They are not!

Recent studies show that such ordinary and trifling irritations can create a number of psychological and physical problems. Shockingly, these small "daily life hassles" can create more stress-related illnesses than major crises such as divorce, loss of a job, or a move to a new community.[1] We automatically allow for the big changes in our lives, but we often don't even want to mention the minor problems.

Stepparents choose their spouses. They choose their friends. They even choose the people they share a cup of coffee with, but they don't, in any meaningful sense, choose the children they find themselves living with. On the other hand, neither do children choose their new stepparents. Yet stepparents and their stepchildren are expected to share a roof, meals, and holidays. They are expected to share a lifetime! After the honeymoon, when this forced closeness first begins to affect both adults and children, uncomfortable feelings and interactions start to take place, often revolving around the "dailiness" of life.

"There's some things that just get on my nerves and I think, well, can I stand this or am I going to make them change? Like wasting toilet paper. That just bothers me to no end."

Karen, 43, Wisconsin

"I can't stand it when my stepson Darren chews with his mouth open. When I tell him about it, he says 'I do it all week at home, and nobody ever says anything to me about it.' Suddenly I'm the bad guy."

Beverly, 22, New Jersey

"My daughter, Jenny, had just turned 13 and had just started her periods. She was a very emotional child in the first place and so everything magnified with her. She had always slept with her cat, but, when we moved into my new husband's house after getting married, here she was in this strange house, and the cat was not allowed to be in her room. That was the very first big mistake."

JoAnne, 55, Arkansas

Banned cats, wasted toilet paper, chewing with mouths open. Small problems? Not at all.

- Why does he lick his fingers after he eats?
- Why does he forget to flush the toilet?
- Why does she refuse to make her own bed?
- Why are there crumbs on the carpet in front of the TV?
- Why did she leave dirty dishes in the sink?
- Why does he sneer at the chicken casserole I made?
- Why does she drive my car and then leave my gas tank on empty?

Why, why, why? Why don't they know what my needs are? Why are they driving me crazy?

As the small problems of living together begin to fester and build, stepparents often feel guilty. They feel that they shouldn't say anything. It seems easier to repress feelings entirely.

Sarah, an actress, married a self-employed professional who had custody of his pre-teen daughter, Melanie. Sarah had no children of her own. On the surface, Sarah's life was easier than that of most new stepparents. Because money was no problem, it was possible for Sarah to hire a full-time housekeeper to cook, care for the house, and take Melanie to school. Nevertheless, even without the difficulties of having to take care of a step-daughter on a daily basis, Sarah experienced many of the same frustrations as stepmothers who have no outside household help.

"At first everything looked good. On a day-to-day basis, it has been more difficult. We still have a full-time *au pair* which, of course, makes a night-and-day kind of difference. It means we can have somewhat of a night life. I can pop off to an audition at the last minute and I don't have to get up early to take her to school on a regular basis. So that has been a great plus, but the day-to-day has gotten harder, and I have a lot of guilt about it. The TV blaring, the records playing loud. A lot of times it's like I can't wait until she goes to bed. How fast can I insist that she do it? I spent a year in therapy, and a lot of time was spent on my relationship with her."

Sarah, 34, New York

When such irritations are suppressed, they may come out with more force later. During the "settling in period," it is easy to begin personalizing annoying things that others do. We sometimes believe that our stepchildren are deliberately trying to hurt us.

- "She hates me, or she wouldn't do that."
- "He's just doing that to get to me."
- "She wants me out of here, so she's going to make certain my life is miserable."

She *purposely* didn't give me my message. She *wants* to cause problems for me. She's *trying* to destroy my life.

As stepparents, we must approach problems openly and quickly. We must find solutions that are mutually acceptable. And we must form a United Front to give both ourselves and our new family the stability and security that it needs to become strong.

Some stepparents feel that it is immature to express small complaints. They feel that if they overlook the "little things," they will be able to rise above them. This approach does not work. At the start of a new marriage, everyone will have problems, everyone will have complaints, everyone will find something or somebody irritating. *It's guaranteed.*

Complaints, once expressed, need to be listened to and given serious consideration by the other members of the family. Can something be done about a given problem? Can a compromise be worked out? Although love is not essential when a family blends, the working out of daily problems and irritations is.

There is no "right" answer or "correct" solution to most of the "little" problems encountered in stepfamily living. For the most part, it does not really matter *how* parents resolve them. What is important is that parents *do* resolve them and that they do so together, as a "united" couple.

Structured Communication between husband and wife is important in resolving the major conflicts, but it is also important to use it in dealing with all the small irritations that come up as families blend. Prior to the marriage ceremony, prospective stepparents were considered dates or guests. Now they are permanent fixtures. Differences in how things are done become more apparent. Stepparents have to exercise more authority because they now have more responsibility.

Coping with change can be difficult from the stepchild's point of view as well.

"At Mom's house, we can eat anywhere—in our bedrooms, in front of the TV, wherever. At Dad's, no food can leave the dining room or kitchen."

"At Dad's, we can make a peanut butter sandwich if we don't like the dinner. At Mom's place, we have to eat the dinner and try a little of everything even if it doesn't smell good."

"Mom makes our beds at home. At Dad's, we have to make our own."

After remarriage, different ways of doing things in the two households are accentuated, and the children may not like the results. They will almost certainly compare the two homes and complain about those differences that work, in their own minds, to their disadvantage.

Yet this required adaptation will not hurt them. Throughout life, we are called upon to "shift gears" in different situations and environments. We must learn to adapt to the people we're with, to the places we visit, to the new challenges that confront us.

We, as parents, must set the rules for our own households. We need to tell our children: "We know it's difficult moving between two families, but when you're here, this is how we do things." The children will adapt, and chances are it will help them later in life when they confront new and different situations and lifestyles. Learning to adapt often proves to be one of the greatest rewards of stepfamily living.

TRIANGLES

When we begin to blend our families together, it is important for us to form a "family circle"—a home where everyone is both *accepted* and *accepting*. One of the major roadblocks to achieving this "circle" is the formation of "triangles."

In some ways, blended family triangles are like romantic triangles. There are two persons who are closely involved with each other and another person in an outside position. At times, the configuration may change. Roles—and loyalties—may shift.

The initial formation of a triangle cannot be controlled, but the way in which it is handled after it occurs can make or break a marriage.

Michele's Story

One of our respondents, Michele, 42, faced a difficult situation, a blending triangle, shortly after her remarriage. As she began telling us about it, she was anxious to make certain that we fully understood the background of her situation.

"My husband got custody of his 15 year old daughter Amy right after the divorce and raised her all by himself. She's lived with him all her life. So I was the one who came into the home where they lived together. When we first married, Don and I were happy together and Amy, a darling girl, always saw the happiness. She was only with us a few weeks before she went off to camp. When she came back after six weeks, it was a day and night switch, an incredible change. I tried to be the good mother, but whatever I did for her, she would destroy. I got her a checking account. What does she do? She bounces one check after another. I gave her free rein with my car, and she wrecked it within one month. The presents I bought for her—she conveniently lost them. The cookies I made for her—she wouldn't eat them. I mean the kid lived on sugar and she wouldn't eat cookies? So I'm thinking—well, I better give up this tactic. Obviously anything I do for her is not going to be accepted. And then I finally start feeling: 'What's the use? What *is* the use?'"

Michele said she "hates to argue" and is not the "arguing type," but she became so desperate that she tried harder and harder to get her husband to intervene in the situation. As the focus of the interview shifted from her stepdaughter Amy to her husband Don, it became more and more difficult for Michele to control her emotions. Twice during the interview, we suggested that the situation might be too painful to talk about, but Michele felt that she *needed* to talk about it.

"One incident really says it. One Sunday morning I got up and went out to get the newspaper, and I went by Amy's room. Two boys were in there sleeping. She wasn't with them. She was in another room. So I went up to wake Don—he was still in a dead sleep—and said, 'Don, there are two boys in Amy's room.' The first thing he said—and this was within two seconds of waking up—was, 'Why did you look?' WHY DID I LOOK? There were comings and goings through the house all night—all kinds of queers and freaks. Don would never believe it. And when my car was damaged, she wasn't even grounded. Don just doesn't want to see what she does. He doesn't want to know that there are problems. He doesn't like problems. It's like—'Don't bother me with the facts; *there is no problem!*'"

When confronted with the "triangle," Michele went through three predictable stages:

1. Trying very hard to make things better.
2. Ignoring the problems.
3. Giving up.

"I tried everything. I tried to be the good mother—always home when she got home from school, involved in school activities, joined the PTA. That didn't work. Then I tried just ignoring it, letting Don take care of the problem. That didn't work because, to Don, there was no problem. I tried not to think about it, but it was always there. Amy kept telling me, 'Dad can divorce you, but he can't divorce me,' and that's what it came down to."

Shortly thereafter, Don and Michele separated, and Michele filed for divorce.

"Amy knew from the start she was in the position of power. I sometimes wonder, could I have done anything more? But I don't think so. I tried so hard."

Michele, 42, Texas

In this situation, we have a shifting triangle. When Michele and Don married, they had a few weeks of happiness, but Amy felt left out. She began to view Michele as the "other woman." Amy was not interested in forming a "family circle" with her father and Michele. She wanted to be the only "love" interest in her father's life.

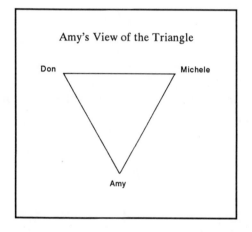

Amy was disturbed by the situation. Her father had raised her. Their bond had always been strong. Amy was not willing to share her father with another woman. She acted to strengthen the bond between herself and her father—at Michele's expense. Amy was successful. Her father did not stop her. He *allowed* the formation of a blended family triangle. Amy was now Michele's "other woman." "Dad can divorce you, but he can't divorce me."

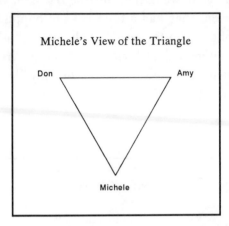

The marriage could not continue unless Don broke the triangle by choosing Michele, by recognizing the absolute necessity of developing a United Front with his wife in the face of his daughter's destructive behavior. A blended family "circle" could not now be constructed until *after* the existing triangle had been demolished.

Since Don did not do this, the marriage dissolved. The triangle was broken only when Michele left and filed for divorce. A family circle *was* finally formed—but it included only Don and Amy.

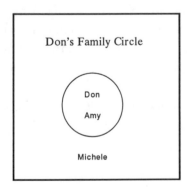

Who is going to stick together? Who is going to be the "odd man out?" If the parent and child band together, the stepparent has no power or authority.

The cause of Don and Michele's divorce was already present, in seminal form, at the outset of their relationship. When a stepfamily experiences problems, the following questions need to be asked:

- Who is ganging up on whom?
- Who is forming a coalition?
- Who is left out?

In strong blended families, coalitions are between the two parents or between the children when they join together as a team to negotiate with Mom and Dad. When generational lines are crossed, unhealthy coalitions are formed. Don and Amy ended up with their own family circle, but, in the future, there will be problems for Amy, as well as Don, when either of them seeks to form another relationship. Power struggles create chaos in the family. If a husband and wife don't stick together, the game is ultimately "no win" for everyone.

Ramona's Story

Another respondent, Ramona, 26, had no idea what she was getting into when she married Gary, 40. Before marriage, their relationship had been a very happy one.

"Stepchildren don't do the same things before marriage that they do afterwards. Before marriage, everything was great. His girls looked at me as an older sister—like I was a big senior woman and they were freshmen. 'Boy, she's hip. Boy, she knows what's going on. She's got neat friends. She's got neat clothes. She's cool.' I was 26 and they were teenagers. They thought I was awesome."

When Ramona's role changed from girlfriend to wife, she suddenly found herself in enemy territory.

"As soon as I got married to their dad, they suddenly thought I was trash, the worst scum that ever walked the earth. The oldest one, Leslie, wrote her dad a letter from college calling me every name in the book and saying that all he wants me for is sex, and why does he need that when he has her? She kept saying she's his *real* family, and, basically: 'Choose me or her.' She and her sister wreaked havoc in our family that first year. They had incredible power over my husband. They were extremely jealous and downright nasty. There were so many demands—things like, 'If you don't take us to dinner with you alone, Dad, then we're not going to have anything to do with you anymore.' It's not just that they're standing over there saying, 'I've got the power,' it's that they break you down so much that you lose power. All of a sudden you end up screaming and yelling at each other."

As time went on, Ramona and Gary's situation grew even more turbulent.

"Leslie saw me more and more as the 'other woman.' She even told me that she was having sex dreams about her dad. I knew it was to shock me, but I still believed that it was true. She also stole lingerie of mine. She and her dad would spend hours in the bedroom talking. She felt that he belonged to her, and she looked at me as a rival. She thought that she could break up our relationship. She tried and hoped to get her dad to choose again, to choose her over me."

At first Leslie seemed to be winning.

"I was starting to have delusions that maybe my husband and his daughter were—maybe there was—an incestual relationship. He would go up to where she was going to school, take her out to dinner, and not come home till 11 o'clock. I'd say, 'Well, where have you been?

What have you been doing?' 'Well, having dinner.' 'For four hours?'
'Leslie and I can spend an incredible amount of time together.' 'Four
hours?' And they were drinking and having dinner and yakking it up,
and I felt really like that was competition. I know she wants him.
There's no doubt in my mind about that. She's come out and said so.
And I felt that he couldn't place her as what she was—that she was his
daughter. I don't think he had sexual desire for her or that he had ever
engaged in a sexual relationship with her, but I do believe he had a
hard time putting her in the right place in his mind. 'She's my daughter.
I really shouldn't be out barhopping with her. I've got a wife at
home.'"

Eventually, following a marriage-threatening blowup, Ramona and Gary sought counseling in an effort to improve the
situation. Slowly Gary came to realize that he had "given" his
daughter the power to abuse his wife, that he had in fact "aban-
doned" his wife in the face of his daughter's angry feelings of
displacement. He "rechose" Ramona and, together, "united,"
they began to rebuild their own relationship.

"Both of us have to be willing to let *us* be in power and not let the kids
be in power. That's the key. It's been a long process for Gary to come
around to that and not let the girls push his buttons all the time. Even
now, when we go on vacation, they'll say, 'How can you go with her
and leave us at home. You're spending *our* money.' But we just go
anyway. Their needs should not be denied, but they should not be in
control of our relationship, either."

Though Ramona and Gary have gone through difficult times
with each other, the situation is beginning to improve. Seeking
counseling and forming a United Front saved their marriage.
The way Gary has now learned to handle his children has
strongly affected the way Ramona responds to them. She is beginning to view them in a more positive way, and the marriage
itself is much happier. In retrospect, Ramona regrets only that

they waited so long to begin working on the problem as a couple.
The delay itself had costs.

"We just had our sixth anniversary, and we said, 'WE LASTED!'—like it
was a miracle. But the problem did zap a lot of the passion out of our
relationship. When you've been fighting constantly for five long years,
it just zaps a lot out of you."
Ramona, 32, Washington

Michele, Don, and Amy had a triangular problem relationship. In a sense, Amy won because Michele, her stepmother,
finally left, and Amy then had her father all to herself. For a
fifteen-year-old girl, however, this was not a healthy outcome.
Amy would have benefited more, in her own future relationships, if Michele and Don had formed a United Front and had
given Amy what she needed rather than what she wanted. The
family would have remained stable, and Amy would have been
able to see the model of a marriage that worked.

Michele felt that the poor relationship with Amy was her
fault, and she felt guilty because of it. In no way, though, did
Ramona feel guilty! She demanded that she be treated with respect and courtesy and that her husband form a United Front
with her against the girls' ongoing mistreatment of her.

Michele and Don got a divorce. Ramona and Gary came
close, but instead they resolved their problems, and today they
do have a happier relationship. The differing results for these
two women are no accident. Stories like theirs were repeated
time and again by survey respondents from across the country.
Unfortunately—and unnecessarily—the "Micheles" of stepfamilies almost always leave the relationship because they feel so
hopeless, believing that things can never be different.

Things *can* be different, *can* be better. The key to creating a
remarriage that lasts lies in developing and maintaining a
United Front with your partner.

SUCCESSFULLY COPING WITH "BLENDING" CONFLICTS

Blended families are the most complex form of family structure we have in American society today. Couples and their children must deal with several stages of the "living together" cycle all at once. It's worse than juggling apples and oranges. It's more like juggling eggs and dynamite. There are so many family unit fragments involved that a Humpty Dumpty syndrome emerges: Can all the king's horses and all the kings men ever put this family together again?

Unlike the parents in first marriages, men and women in second marriages do not stay married *because* of the children. Rather, the children are the most divisive force in the marriage.

In both nuclear families and stepfamilies, children often play one parent against the other. Yet, in a nuclear family, if a threat to the family occurs, these same children are likely to do everything in their power to keep their parents together. In stepfamilies, the situation is very different. The children often wish that the new marriage will break up. They often think that, if it does, their two natural parents will be reunited.[2] If we, as parents, can come to realize that our children do not always want our new marriage to last and may seek to destroy it, then we can unite to make sure that they do not succeed. This is difficult for us to do since we are sensitive to our children's feelings and hate to see them unhappy. We repeatedly ask ourselves the question: "How will this affect our children's lives?"

The answer is a very positive one. If we—and our children—can successfully work our way though the "aftershock" stage of remarriage, the results will be positive for all of us. Learning to live in a blended family environment can be a healthy experience for children. They will discover very quickly that no one is perfect, that everyone has flaws, but they will also learn that the ability to compromise and adapt are useful skills in all aspects of our lives.

If our children can discover these facts early, they—and we!—will have learned one of the basic rules of "happily-ever-aftering."

5

New Brothers, New Sisters

"We have yours—mine—ours. They have been taught they are brother and sister—no 'half' sister, no 'step' brother. The girls all adore their older 'brother'."

Julia, 39, Tennessee

"We all live under the same roof, and they regard themselves as brothers and sisters."

Irene, 33, Louisiana

"All eight kids get along pretty good—even with six of them in one bedroom and two more on the living room couch. We're cramped, but when they get together on Friday nights, it's all instant excitement. You can't get anybody to bed because they're all so happy to see each other again."

Paula, 27, California

The new stepfamily scene can be fun. Kids like a family: the holidays, the traditions, the hustle and bustle, the noise and activity. They enjoy the "kid" things they do together: going out for pizza, having picnics at the beach, celebrating each other's birthdays. Relating to adults all the time can be a strain. Having other kids around takes the pressure off. It's more relaxing for children. It's more fun. There aren't as many demands and obligations. Other kids won't say: "You can't go play till you clean your room." Other kids don't care if you stay up till midnight watching "Nightmare on Elm Street, Part 27" on the VCR. They're in this whole thing with you.

NEW FRIENDS

Many of us feel that the "new family" is a wonderful gift that we have given our children. Only twelve percent of our survey respondents believed that their children and stepchildren did not get along very well with each other. *Fifty percent* of our parents and stepparents were extremely positive about the situation. They stated that the stepsiblings had a relationship that was "very good" or "couldn't be better." They felt that stepbrothers and stepsisters had enriched the lives of their own children. Though there were a few negative anecdotes about relationships between stepsiblings reported in our interviews and questionnaires, most of the stories were positive ones—moving accounts of children helping other children.

"It was love at first sight with all four children. They just fell in love with each other. In our family portrait, you'd never be able to guess whose child was whose. We are a family. No one in this town ever realized we were step. I mean, we all looked alike. We looked like a family, and we acted like a family, and they all had the same last name. The four children never acted like anything but flesh and blood siblings."

Joanna, 48, Virginia

"The two stepsisters have a wonderful, unique relationship considering they're the same age. They get along great. I'm amazed by it actually."

Susan, 35, Washington

Many of us, as stepparents, are "amazed" at how well our children and stepchildren get along together. The children may have serious conflicts with us, their stepfathers and stepmothers, but, at the same time, will get along beautifully with their stepbrothers and stepsisters. The step*family* scene is often less intimidating and more appealing than the step*parent* scene.

"When we first met each other, his kids wouldn't even look at me, but they related well to my kids. It's still difficult for them to relate to me, but they all love each other."

Glenna, 34, California

"I got to dread the weekends because I knew I was going to get walked on by his kids: no help, lying, talking back. The kids themselves always got along well though. They played games together and went places together. They were just always close. No rivalry or jealousy whatsoever between the girls. We could go on vacations together with no problems. The girls shared clothes and makeup and slept together."

Eleanor, 53, Florida

Sometimes even closer bonds develop between stepsiblings. When parents marry, their children may develop deep, lifelong friendships. They may grow to love each other. They might even end up married!

"He had sixteen kids. I had four. My oldest daughter and his oldest son got married."

Ruth, 54, South Dakota

ROMANTIC OR SEXUAL ATTRACTIONS

Usually stepbrothers and stepsisters think of each other as siblings, but sometimes the relationship is more than a friendship or familial bond. Romantic or sexual attractions between stepbrothers and stepsisters is an area that we, as parents, need to be alert to. Romantic interactions can be enriching and positive. Some stepsiblings actually do end up married to one another. At other times, the situation is *not* positive.

When families blend, new family constellations form. Personal space is shared, yet biological family taboos are not automatically present. Children who are not related are suddenly thrown into close proximity with each other. Most of the time this does not create a problem. The stepsiblings themselves are inhibited by personal modesty and by the small irritating habits in others which are always a part of living together. In other situations, feelings that stepsiblings have for one another can be difficult to control. The children have not grown up together and do not view each other as "brother" or "sister." The incest taboo is not as strong. The resulting behavior may not be appropriate.

Children and adolescents are reluctant to tell parents about sexual feelings or physical interactions with a stepbrother or stepsister. Instead, they may tell a friend or a counselor. Some have even written to Ann Landers.[1] Others don't tell anyone at all.

Rosharon's stepfamily experience was an unfortunate one:

"As a young child, I was very affectionate. I loved to hug family and friends. I was someone who would walk up to strangers and ask for money for a drink or hot dog. One day, my loving behavior changed dramatically. I was raped by my two stepbrothers. They told me that they were going to play a game. I loved to play games, but I had never played any games like this before. I was seven at the time and didn't understand. My two stepbrothers were eleven, and I'm positive they knew sex was wrong. I asked an older friend, 'What is it when a boy lays on top of you and goes up and down?' She was shocked. I told her about the boys and myself and all the different places we had played our 'games.' She told me to scream and kick if they tried to have sex with me again. I did, but then they forced themselves on me. They said that it was a punishment. I remember crying as I went to the bathroom because they had cut me a little. . . . One year later I moved to New Orleans to live with my dad. The court said I could visit my mother every other weekend—if neither of the boys was in the house."

Rosharon, 21, Louisiana

As parents, we want to make our home a safe, secure place for all the children. The thought of physical trespassing or sexual relations between children is frightening, yet we must be alert to this possibility. Five percent of the parents in our survey who have or who had stepsiblings in their family reported that there had been at one time a romantic or sexual attraction between stepbrothers and stepsisters.

"Briefly there were problems between my 17-year-old girl and his twenty-year-old son. He made advances to her. He then moved out of state. It happened only one time. My daughter told me about it."

Lauren, 27, Maryland

"Barry assaulted Kimberley one night when she was asleep. After that, when the boys came to visit, Kimberley and I moved to a motel for the weekend."

Martina, 42, Texas

"My son had a little trouble with his stepsister. She was a little more worldly, and she did make a pass at him once. That really upset him."

Arlene, 54, California

Romantic or sexual attractions can cover a wide spectrum of situations. Girls initiate relationships with stepbrothers; boys make advances toward stepsisters. In addition to stepbrother/stepsister attractions, nearly three percent of our questionnaire responses noted that there had been sexual interactions between brothers and stepbrothers. In many of these cases, the boys were quite young.

"A sexual experience did arise between my spouse's son and my youngest son."
Cindy, 37, Massachusetts

"We found the seven-year-old boys in inappropriate sexual behavior."
Dorothy, 30, South Carolina

"The older boys had sexual play and fondling of each other."
Bob, 34, Georgia

In almost all of the reported cases of sexual interactions between stepsiblings, parents became aware of the situation early and took steps to prevent it from becoming a larger problem. Discussions were held, and parents were open.

"We are open about sexual matters and were able to diffuse it through honesty. It was clearly inappropriate behavior."
Roberta, 49, California

Children need to know their boundaries. While feelings will often be there, inappropriate *behavior* is in another sphere. Sexual play, especially among younger children, is not in itself an indication that anything is wrong. Children are fascinated by their own bodies and by the bodies of others, so parents should be careful not to let their own fears cause them to overreact. At the same time, it's reasonable for parents to let their children know that some parts of one's body are private.

JEALOUSY AMONG STEPSIBLINGS

Competition is common among brothers and sisters. All children fight and compete at times. In a stepfamily, rivalry is to be expected, but sometimes it is intensified because of the circumstances. Twenty-nine percent of our respondents stated that competition was a frequent problem between the children and stepchildren in their family.

When children live together, whether permanently or just during visits, they can't avoid having to share space, food, possessions, and even people. Often they are afraid there isn't going to be enough to go around—enough bedrooms or ice cream, enough toys or money—and, especially, enough love. Sharing with new people can create jealousy. Children want to feel important; they want to feel bigger and better than others. They want to be "the best" in Mom's or Dad's eyes. Stepsiblings threaten this desired perception. They try to steal the limelight. They might be prettier, smarter, or more athletic. If they live with Dad or Mom, it might even seem that they are loved more. Jealousy quickly turns to anger if children feel that their new brothers or sisters are being treated better or are getting more. The words "jealousy" and "competition" appeared repeatedly in our survey responses:

"Jealousy is a problem. One is afraid the other will get something he didn't get."
Barbara, 24, South Carolina

"There's competition and alienation and defensiveness. Each set of children says: '*We* are going here with dad or mom' or 'Mom gave *us* candy and she said we don't have to share with *you*.'"

Marilyn, 30, Colorado

"My stepchildren are sometimes jealous that my children live in a better house, have a better car, etc. But it was their choice to live with their mother."

Glenna, 34, California

In our personal situation (authors Jim and Mary Ann), we had a special challenge in this area. When we married, Jim's son and Mary Ann's son were both fourteen, and Jim's daughter and Mary Ann's daughter were both eleven. Before marriage, we thought this would be an advantage. In no way were we prepared for the competition and insecurities the situation created. All of the children had lost their special and unique places in the family. Birth orders and family positions were rearranged. Brad was no longer the oldest. Heidi was no longer the youngest. Jilian was not the "only" daughter. Mark was not the "only" son. Identities shifted and changed. Brad had a stepbrother in the same class at school. Jilian had a sister who was the same age. Everyone had to share a home, cars, food, parents, and love. Competition ran rampant—over anything and everything. The question of who would get that last piece of pizza led to open warfare. The pizza was not the real issue. The children feared that there wasn't enough of anything—or anybody!—to go around.

Mark, Brad, Heidi, and Jilian are all close to each other now, and we believe that they are more adaptable in other situations in their lives because of this experience. At the same time, we could have made it so much easier for them, and for us, if we had discussed the potential problem areas more fully before we married.

Usually the parent becomes the focus of intersibling competition. It's hard for children to see their mother or father living with other children and giving affection and gifts to those children.

"My husband's oldest daughter is a problem. She doesn't feel that my daughter should get any time or attention from Dad."
Mildred, 60, Virginia

"They are constantly fighting over toys and 'Dad.' The stepson won't listen and physically tortures my son."
Joyce, 29, Ohio

"The main problem between the children is attention. The stepchildren feel their father loves the children who live at home more than them."
Dixie, 37, Louisiana

Sometimes stepsibling jealousy erupts into open hostility. Twenty-six percent of our respondents felt that their children and stepchildren demonstrated frequent hostility toward each other. In 1987, Thomas Mann did an extensive statistical analysis, comparing differences in children's aggressiveness in stepfamilies and nondivorced families. He found that children in stepfamilies were "significantly more aggressive."[2] If aggression and hostility between children become too extreme, the children become dividers in the family; feelings are polarized, and battle camps form.

"There is lots of jealousy. The children have played my husband and me against each other, and our marriage has almost broken up because of it."
Marcia, 34, California

"There's constant fighting and getting the others in trouble. There seems to be hate toward one another and too many times where everyone takes sides."

Brenda, 24, Ohio

"There's fighting and teasing all the time and tension when they are all together. They try to work us against each other."

Jeff, 41, Utah

Just as parents undergo emotional turmoil when their children and stepchildren don't get along, so do the children. When problems are serious between children and their stepsiblings, the children often withdraw from the situation.

"My oldest stepchild is extremely jealous of my oldest daughter. At first I talked a lot to my children. I would not allow mine to hit them. In the end, I just didn't care. After one month, my stepdaughter moved back to her grandparents."

Kate, 38, California

"Jealousy between children is a major problem. The stepchildren want to deny being part of a stepfamily and don't visit our home any longer— at their request."

Sally, 35, Virginia

"My stepson is openly hostile to my daughter and also jealous. She lives with her grandmother now."

Dawn, 36, Pennsylvania

Hostility grew so strong in one stepfamily that a young teenager was afraid to even visit her father when her stepbrother was present.

"Phil thinks my dad treats me better than him; Dad punishes him more. Phil told me once, 'Someday I'm going to kill you.' I'm scared to go over there, even though I don't think he'd really do anything."
Jan, 14, New Mexico

A few parents express the view that the children will eventually grow up, and, when that happens, jealousy will simply go away. Other parents note that this does not necessarily happen.

"I have found that even if you have an adult stepchild it can be as severe a problem as stepchildren in the home. My son is 30, and my husband's children are older. They are still jealous of my son if they know he's here a lot."
Lynn, 61, Minnesota

WHEN CHILDREN FIGHT

How should we handle jealousy among stepsiblings? The parents and stepparents in our survey used five different methods. Each of the five can be effective. Different situations often call for different strategies.

Work for Equality

Since children are so prone to suspect unequal treatment, many parents strive to be fair to all the children and not give any of them priority treatment.

"The children were all treated equally and got along with no problems."
Gail, 64, Florida

"The kids were young when we married and were raised just alike. No problems between them at all. They are just OUR KIDS. We are just A FAMILY."

Neil, 47, Florida

"What you do for one, you must do for the other. Or don't tell the other!"

Dan, 39, Louisiana

When anger and aggression erupt, equal treatment can mean equal punishment.

"We find out what is right and show them the difference, then spank them both."

Dan, 39, Louisiana

We give like punishment for all who were involved."

Julia, 45, Wyoming

When some children visit and some live in the home, it can become difficult to treat everyone equally. Yet it is important to do so. When parents treat visiting children like royalty and the children who live in the home like commoners, the scene will be set for feelings of resentment. Parents will be more successful if they try to give all the children their share of parental attention even when visiting children are present.

Try to Be Impartial

Two-thirds of our survey respondents emphasized the importance of letting the children work out their own problems. Many of them were adamant in their feelings that taking sides creates even more problems.

"Brian, my son, was just one year younger than Karen, and they were real good friends when Jack and I were dating. After we married, Brian got a job in Texas and Karen decided that she would go down there, too, and stay with him. After one week, she came back just madder than all get out. They couldn't live together under the same roof, even without the parents. Of course, they then both wanted to tell us their story and what a bad guy the other one was. We just didn't listen to either one of them. We said that it wasn't any of our business, that they'd have to work it out. They're friends again now, but they never tried living together again either."

Betty, 47, Iowa

"I usually have to walk away. Once I stepped in, and the oldest boy took it out on me, defending his natural brother."

Brenda, 24, Ohio

"If there's no blood spilled, they must settle it themselves. They usually go to their separate rooms first, then get lonely and come out to talk to each other."

Shirley, 34, California

If we side with our stepchildren, our own children might resent us. If we side with our children, our stepchildren are very likely to feel this is because of the natural parent bond. When children have to work through their own conflicts, they are more likely to resolve them and, at the same time, not feel hostile toward the adult.

Encourage Discussion and Introspection

A large number of parents felt that it was essential to stimulate discussion between the children. Children need to be urged to look at themselves and their own actions instead of claiming, "But she did this to *me*," or the ever-popular "He started it!"

They need to be told that they have to live together and that they have to work it out.

"We try to let them work it out, but we don't allow cruelty. We also try to discuss what prompted it."
Dorothy, 30, South Carolina

Some of the parents who used this method emphasize that while they tried not to interfere with *how* the problems were resolved, they did attempt to help the children get to the root of the conflict.

Directly Intervene

One-fourth of our survey respondents believed in direct intervention when their children had problems.

"I send them each to their room and make them write ten things they like about each other. Then they each have to read what the other wrote."
Anne, 43, Louisiana

"I make whoever is fighting (right or wrong) sit real close to each other on the couch for fifteen minutes. They usually end up laughing."
Anita, 49, New York

Many of these parents stressed the importance of a positive resolution of problems between stepsiblings.

"We sit down, hear both sides, and then they 'kiss and make up.' "
Kate, 36, Florida

"I separate them or talk to them, tell them they are sisters and what they are fighting about isn't as important as family love."

Barbara, 24, South Carolina

"I try to explain that they should love one another and try to accept each other as different people."

Kitty, 36, New York

Make Your Marriage Your Top Priority

One of the most important things that parents can do to help the whole family live happily together is to make their *own* relationship with their husband or wife the cornerstone of family harmony. When parents get along well with each other, their children usually get along also. Our research findings strongly supported this point. In 97 percent of the families where the marriage was the top priority, the children also related well to each other.

In 97% of Remarried Families:
A United Front = Good Stepsibling Relationships

Once again, the United Front is essential. Nowhere is this more important than in the establishment and enforcement of household rules. Two questions parents must resolve together are: (1) what are the children's privileges, and (2) what are their responsibilities. These are the areas of potential inconsistency that cause the most difficulties when children from two families live together.

We *must* be in agreement with our husband or wife on these two critical questions. Together, we need to anticipate the problems and determine our responses. Who does what chores? How is this decided? Will there be curfews? What times for what ages? Should there be dress codes within the house? What level of nudity/semi-nudity is acceptable? Unacceptable? How formal or informal should behavior be at the dinner table? Once the rules for the children have been established and communicated, they will know what to expect and will be less likely to resent their stepsiblings over imagined unfairnesses.

RELATIONSHIPS CHANGE WITH TIME

Many parents told us that it was difficult to assess how their children and stepchildren related to each other because the situation had changed over time. Sometimes relationships had been very good but had changed for the worse.

"All five lived with us. The children actually got along well. They shared and played together. When they fought they pretty much settled it themselves. We would sometimes sit down and have family discussions and air things out. We all seemed happy for about five years or so. I'm not really sure what happened. The kids became teenagers, and relationships started to deteriorate. Somehow a complete line was drawn—yours and mine—two families against one another. My husband and I are now four months into our separation. The children have torn us apart. They do not get along well, and many broken hearts have developed."

Charlotte, 38, Illinois

"When we all lived together and they were in school, the kids all got along great. They stood together against us. After they left home, things changed. They all live close but don't visit or call each other."

Melina, 49, Missouri

In other situations, stepbrothers and stepsisters did not get along well at first but grew closer as the years went by.

"When the children were small, there was normal sibling rivalry, but there is no friction at all now. My adult children are very friendly with their stepbrothers and stepsisters and are role models for the younger children. We all pulled together."

Patricia, 56, Oregon

"He had three, I had three, and we had one together. His second daughter didn't like my first daughter, but the #2 stepdaughter now gets along better with my second daughter than with her own sister. They all live close to us and built their homes on our farm."

Mildred, 60, Virginia

CREATING POSITIVE RELATIONSHIPS

Things do change in all families over time. Distance between children might grow, but usually it does not. The success in child blending reported by our respondents was one of the most positive and encouraging findings in our survey. Parents are doing well in this area.

For most children, having new brothers and sisters appears to be a happy experience. This is true partly because children automatically enjoy other children, but parents are also doing a great deal to foster good stepsibling relationships. They genuinely want their children to get along well together and to build lasting friendships, and they are willing to work hard at treating *all* of the children equally and fairly.

The United Front is the single best tool that we can recommend for creating and maintaining good relationships between stepsiblings. You will know that you are being successful in your approach the first time that the children band together against the common enemy: you, the parents! In our own stepfamily, we were always pleased when this happened since it brought the children closer to each other and, at the same time, demonstrated the basic fairness underlying our treatment of all of them.

If our marriage is strong, our children will get along well with each other. For us, as parents, watching these relationships and friendships evolve is one of the greatest rewards of living in a blended family.

6

The "Other Parent"

We call them our children's "other parents." Sometimes we get along with them. More often we do not. Whether we like it or not, they are a part of our family tree. The men and women they subsequently marry also become part of our divorce-extended family.

In the decades to come, serial marriages are expected to become even more common. More and more children will have an excess of parents, and their family trees will begin to look much like ours.

Our own "tree" is a complex one. Jim's children have a biological father, a biological mother, a stepmother, and an ex-stepfather. Mary Ann's children have a biological mother, a biological father, a stepfather, a stepmother, and an ex-stepmother.

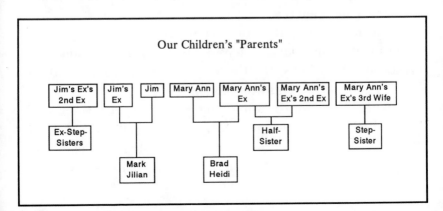

Our Children's "Parents"

When we remarried in 1983, we thought of our family as a nuclear family: a father, a mother, and four kids. We all lived in the same house. The children attended the same school. We went to the same church. We celebrated everyone's birthday as a family group. We referred to Mark, Brad, Heidi, and Jilian as "our kids." We viewed ourselves as a "normal" family. In reality, the kids were not *our* kids. We shared them with their other parents.

We tried not to think about the other parents much, but this proved impossible. They were not mere images which could be thrown away like old photographs. In many different ways, they were a presence—an intrusive presence—in our home. Their phone calls came at all hours. Whatever we were doing had to be dropped to discuss travel plans or other visitation problems. Our Christmases were spent alone or with friends while our children celebrated with them. After visits, the other parents gave the children "messages" to transmit back to us—usually negative ones. There were other interchanges—mostly unpleasant ones. We yelled at each other. We called each other names. We argued endlessly over money and ended up in court when we were unable to resolve the issues on our own. It seemed as if we were infected with a contagious, ongoing anger which we passed back and forth among ourselves. The intensity of their hostility toward us was matched only by the intensity of our hostility toward them. Anger—and shared children—linked us together. It also drained a lot of energy.

For the children, the situation was extremely difficult. They felt caught in the middle. They were tense both before and after visitation. They hated the threats of "going to court" and the never-ending arguments over money.

When Mary Ann's ex-husband got a second divorce and, later, Jim's ex-wife also got another divorce, all four children became even more confused about relationships. A stepmother had now become an ex-stepmother. A stepfather was now an ex-stepfather. Stepparents, it seemed, could be quickly and easily discarded, disposed of like used Kleenex. Loyalties could shift; sides could change overnight. Homes were in a state of flux. Male/female relationships did not seem at all permanent. To our children, instability was becoming the norm. Their recognition of the vulnerability, the fragility, of relationships is still a problem in their lives today, a problem that may continue for years.

For us, their parents, the cost was not as high—nor has it impacted our lives with the same emotional intensity. We were not hurt when our exes had marital problems and divorced a second time. Secretly, we gloated. We felt validated, personally exonerated. *They* were the ones with the problems. Their second divorces were proof of what we had been telling ourselves all along. No one could get along with them!

Of course, it really wasn't that simple. In reality, uniting against the enemy, the "evil" exes, added a sense of unity to *our* new marriage. It was the two of us against them! A siege—the belief that our home was under attack—decidedly heightened our feelings of excitement and romance. This combat mentality led to feelings of high drama in our minds, and we failed to notice the effects of our soap opera world on our children.

Ultimately, we had to recognize that the price of war was much too high. It hurt us in our roles as parents, and it truly harmed our children. They were the innocent victims caught in our crossfire. It took us years to realize that, regardless of our anger, we had to make peace with the children's other parents.

THE WAR OF THE EXES

In our interviews and questionnaires, we found that our respondents, like us, often lived in battle zones. Ex-husbands and ex-wives were the people they loved to hate!

"I would love to dance on my ex-husband's grave!"

Karen, 47, Kansas

"I hate my husband's ex and wish she were dead or seriously handicapped."

Nanette, 32, Iowa

He and I have been civil to one another, but personally I think my wife's ex is a real dweeb."

Jerry, 26, Texas

"I hate my husband's ex. I wouldn't help her save her life. If she were drowning, I wouldn't even throw her a rope."

Ginny, 41, Tennessee

"My husband's ex-wife was a bad wife, a bad mother, and now she's dead—thank goodness!"

Diane, 42, New York

Webster's defines the word "ex" as: "former, away from, out of." "Former" or "away from" implies something that no longer has an impact on our lives. Seldom is this the case with ex-husbands or ex-wives. In our survey, seventy-one percent of the men and women in remarriages had negative feelings about their *own* ex-husbands or ex-wives. Sixty-three percent of our respondents held negative feelings about their *spouses'* ex-husbands or ex-wives.

The strong emotions are easy to understand. When a marriage dies, a vision dies. It does not really matter who chose to initiate the marital break, how miserable the relationship had become, or who did what to whom. At one time, there had been a dream: two people who believed they could create a happy future together. They loved one another, and they married. They had children, and they dreamed together.

Visions and shattered dreams don't die easily. Images of what "could have been" linger on, haunting our memories for years to come. When an ex-husband or ex-wife remarries, the power of these broken dreams is intensified. A new marriage snatches away the last remnant of the vision and any hope of recapturing the original dream. Remarriage ensures loss just as decisively as death does. Anyone who has been married and whose former spouse has remarried knows this feeling. We remember where we were on the day of the remarriage just as clearly as we remember where we were when John F. Kennedy was assassinated in 1963. Sometimes the mourning and grieving—and anger—go on for years or even decades.

If we are parents in a blended family, our former husbands or former wives will strongly influence our present lives. If we are stepparents, we have to deal with our spouse's former partner—even if that partner is no longer alive. These are remarriage facts, and there is no way we can escape from them.

Our real challenge is to fully realize that we cannot escape, that we cannot simply decide to ignore the situation. Ex-husbands and ex-wives are important relationships from the past, and we need to learn how to live comfortably with this reality. We have to ask ourselves: How can we coexist with our ex-husbands and ex-wives in a way that will not be harmful to us or our children?

The answers are not easy. There are no guarantees, but we can begin by trying to understand the reasons ex-spouse relationships are such an ongoing problem for most of us.

WHY WE FIGHT

The two major areas of warfare between exes are financial differences and child-related frustrations. Both men and women experience these problems. They both find them hard to handle. Yet there are significant differences in the way they react to them. We found that our male respondents' main concern was with money while our female respondents were most concerned about child-related issues. These gender differences were much more pronounced than we would have predicted or anticipated.

Finances

Men are much more affected than women by negative financial interactions or arguments. This is their primary area of disagreement with ex-spouses. For men, financial problems translate directly into a bad relationship with the ex who is, from the male perspective, "responsible" for the problems. This feeling was expressed again and again.

"Our relationship is very strained. After two years and my remarriage, we're still in court regarding child support and the property settlement."
Brad, 39, Washington

"Our relationship is not good. Unless I'm giving her something, she only cares about herself and no one else."
Leroy, 41, Illinois

Men who have financial problems with ex-wives seldom get along well with those ex-wives. The reason for this is clear: re-married men often find themselves under heavy financial pressures—and they greatly resent it.

David, a 53 year old Texas physician, earned $200,000 a year before taxes. His ex-wife and three children received $80,000 a year in child support and alimony payments. When David remarried a woman with two children and had another of his own, he found himself facing financial conflicts. The children from his first marriage continued to make additional financial requests, requests over and above the $80,000 a year he already gave them. David and his new family soon found that they were not living nearly as well as his first family. Even with a very high income, David was financially strapped. His resentment grew and festered more each year.

Kyle, a 46 year old physician in Iowa, made $80,000 a year. He paid $650 a month to his first ex-wife in child support for his two older children. He also paid $1,600 a month in alimony and child support to his second ex-wife and his youngest child. When Kyle married for the third time, his new wife chose to become a homemaker. Thus, Kyle was the sole support of his new family, a wife and stepdaughter.

As the financial pressures built, Kyle fell behind in alimony and child support payments to his second wife. His negative feelings grew so intense that attempts to negotiate the problem proved futile. When the case went to court, the judge was not sympathetic. He not only increased the amount of Kyle's monthly payments but sentenced him to five days in jail as well. In issuing the decision, the District Court judge ruled that:

The financial problem the Respondent now finds himself in is of his own making in that he incurred new obligations. The Court finds that this Respondent did have the ability to satisfy the obligations under the original Decree had he not established a list of priorities placed above the decretal obligations such as meeting the monthly expenses of his present family to the exclusion of the obligation that he owed his prior family. Therefore the Court concludes that the Respondent's failure to pay the obligation set out above was willful. It is further ordered that the Respondent is committed to the County Jail for a period of five days.

Situations such as this are not unusual. Courts are inclined to view the original family, not the stepfamily, as a man's financial priority, and some fathers would rather go to jail than "give in" to the financial demands of their ex-wives. A great deal of media attention has been focused on the belief that the wife's standard of living *goes down* and the husband's standard of living *goes up* after a divorce. The majority of the men in our survey feel that this is not true, especially after remarriage.

Remarried men feel burdened by financial pressures. In many cases, they truly do *not* live as well as their first families. As a result, they focus a great deal of resentment on their ex-wives.

The Children

While finances are the sensitive area for men, the children are the vulnerable zone, the primary area of ex-spouse disagreement, for women. Though we have all heard stories where ex-husbands claim that their former wives use visitation as a weapon, in our survey most women insisted that they did not try to keep their ex-husbands from visiting with their children. On the contrary, these women became upset when their ex-husbands *did not see the children often.* These mothers empathized with their children and feared that the children would feel rejected.

In addition, women often want more time for themselves. When their ex-husbands do not help with child-rearing responsibilities, the mothers have to handle it all themselves.

"He rarely if ever sees his children. As a result, my husband and I never have a weekend alone."

Marilyn, 40, Pennsylvania

"My ex doesn't call or write the kids. We've always made him welcome. He just doesn't care, I suppose. Ex-husbands are nerds."

Rhonda, 31, Texas

"I try to be tolerant of my ex-husband, but he does not take the children often enough so my husband and I can have a bit more time to ourselves. It's just not fair."

Janice, 51, Texas

Most women truly want their children's biological father to participate in the children's lives, but, frequently, this does not happen.

Divorce itself is usually not the culprit. Rather, remarriage is. When a man remarries—or when his ex-wife remarries—he often begins to distance himself from his children. Though this happens slowly at first, the effects tend to grow over the years.

When a man's ex-wife remarries and the children live with her and their new stepfather, the biological father starts to feel like an outsider. He no longer sees himself as the patriarch of a family, an authority figure. It is easier to withdraw than to face the feelings of parental impotency and embarrassment that the situation engenders.

When it is the man himself who remarries, his new wife becomes a significant factor in his relationship with his children and in their relationship with him. In the first years of remarriage, the new kinship probably will run into "aftershock" problems—on both sides of the fence. The new stepmother will have stepchild problems. The new stepchildren will have stepmother problems. As these problems become more burdensome and depressing, many fathers opt to become less involved with the children of their former marriages. The discomfort level is simply too high. The children have become an encumbrance rather than a joy, and these fathers find it easier to create an emotional distance than to deal with the problem directly.

As fathers begin to withdraw, children suffer. As children suffer, former wives grow angry. The entire situation becomes extremely painful—*to everyone.*

WIDENING THE WAR

Though the battles which erupt between ex-husbands and ex-wives are bad enough, the anger-driven combativeness of remarriage does not stop there. Our study clearly shows that when remarried husbands and wives react to ex-spouses they react *as a unit.* Seventy-one percent of our respondents described their relationship with their ex-spouses in negative terms. In most of those cases, the new partners shared the same feelings. If a wife dislikes her ex-husband, her new husband will also dislike him. If a husband fights with his ex-wife, his new wife will most likely fight with her also. A husband becomes angry when his wife is angry. A wife becomes hurt when her husband is hurt.

In our survey, it was almost impossible for a husband or wife to feel positive about an ex if his or her new partner had negative feelings. Biases were passed along from one partner to the other. Once again, it's as if feelings about exes are contagious.

But while fathers and stepmothers, mothers and stepfathers, agree on whether their exes and their partners' exes are "good" or "bad," their explanations as to *why* differ significantly by gender.

Stepfathers vs. Ex-Husbands

The majority of stepfathers have negative feelings about their wives' ex-husbands. The three most common reasons they give for this are:

- My wife's ex-husband is not helpful in handling problems concerning the children, especially financial problems.
- My wife's ex-husband treats her badly.
- My wife's ex-husband does not see the children often enough.

Statistically, when all three factors are present, it is almost certain that the new husband will dislike his wife's ex-husband.

Nearly two-thirds of the stepfathers in our survey reported that they have little direct contact with their wife's former husband. Some men actively avoid situations which might lead to such contact.

"He doesn't acknowledge my existence. I repay the favor."
Jeff, 39, California

"We're not exactly buddies. He resents me, and I don't care for him."
Jack, 32, Texas

"I steer clear of him because I'm afraid I might try to break his scrawny neck."
Don, 30, Kansas

Though stepfathers rarely deal with their wives' ex-husbands directly, they are likely to take action in other ways. Ten percent of our survey responses reported situations where stepfathers either adopted or attempted to adopt their stepchildren.

"My stepdaughter is four years old, and I am attempting an open adoption. But even though the child's father has not seen her in three years, I still need to have his consent and to date he refuses me that right."
Harold, 26, California

"We all met together one day and my new husband, Kurt, asked my ex-husband to release the kids to adoption. He agreed, and Kurt adopted the younger one. But Jenny, who was 14, refused to go along with it, even though she also refused to have anything more to do with her dad because he had rejected her."

JoAnne, 55, Arkansas

"My ex-husband left the area for parts unknown. We haven't seen or heard from him in one and a half years. My daughter has been adopted by her stepfather."

Ginny, 30, Washington

In other situations, stepfathers encouraged their stepchildren to make a complete break with the biological father.

"Kelli's father had put her through this emotional abuse for years. She had been trying to dump that load for a long time, and I'd like to think that I had been a help there. First by being an example to her that not every man on the face of the earth is scum. And second by talking with her about the problem. Not that I would come down the stairs each morning saying, 'Your old man is a scumbag,' but if she would bring up something he had done, I would agree with her: 'Yes, that wasn't a good thing to do,' or, 'You have a right to be upset about that.' He kept laying guilt trips on her, and when he finally asked her, 'Should I start telling people I don't have a child anymore?' she answered, 'If you'd like to, you may.' It took courage for her to do that, but she did it."

Don, 30, Kansas

Both in our study and in others, a common pattern emerges. After a remarriage, ex-husbands without custody are apt to withdraw from the new family. A recent study at the University of Pennsylvania found that 42 percent of the children of divorce had not even seen their fathers during the previous year. Remarriage validates the finality of a divorce and sometimes even blunts former paternal feelings. Ex-husbands who do not have custody tend to see the ex-wife's new family, the new household, as a closed door. Often the unfortunate result is the father's withdrawal from his children as well, his severance of a continuing relationship with *anyone* from the former family.[1] This creates problems not only with ex-wives and with children but also with stepfathers.

If an ex-husband sees the children less often and does not take an active part in their lives, the stepfather begins to resent him. At this point, many stepfathers take action. Some of them urge their stepchildren to break off the relationship with their biological father altogether. Others initiate adoption proceedings.

This pattern, which is common among ex-husbands and stepfathers, is very rare among ex-wives and stepmothers.

Stepmothers vs. Ex-Wives

As with stepfathers and ex-husbands, negative feelings are the norm for stepmothers and ex-wives. Women, however, handle these feelings much differently. Only one percent of the women in our survey had attempted to adopt their stepchildren. Only three percent had urged their stepchildren to cut off the relationship with the other parent. One reason for this difference is that biological mothers rarely allow their children to be adopted by a stepmother. Among our survey respondents, adoption by a stepmother occurred in fewer than one percent of the families and, in those reported situations, the biological mother was either dead or institutionalized.

Also, women do not tend to withdraw from their children even if they do not have custody. As a part of our research, we attended a meeting of the group "Mothers Without Custody" and talked with many of the mothers. Although these women did not have custody and were not raising their children on a day-to-day basis, they still chose involvement over withdrawal and were a strong, continuing presence in their children's lives. In no way did they attempt to distance themselves emotionally from the children.

"I figured if she wanted my husband so bad she could have the kids, too. I visit the kids every other weekend, and we have a great relationship. I dress up and we go out to dinner or shopping. Their stepmother just sits there looking mad—and tired. So what. She deserves it. Giving custody to my ex-husband and his new wife gave me a rest during the tough teenage years. Now I get along with the kids better than they do. It was the best decision I ever made."

Helene, 48, Massachusetts

"Their stepmother doesn't take good care of them, so I have to stay closely involved. When they come for a visit, their suitcases are a mess—dirty underwear, everything thrown in and wrinkled. She doesn't even bother to do their laundry or mend their torn clothes. I finally wrote her a letter telling her just what I thought of her."

Joan, 46, Iowa

Incidents such as these are extremely disconcerting to the stepmother who is "raising" someone else's children. She highly resents the biological mother's intrusion.

"It's very easy to make your biological mother your good mother and your stepmother your bad mother. My stepdaughter Karin lives with us, but she's in pursuit of her mom. It's that whole philosophy of distance/pursuer. In our town everyone walks to high school, so Karin walks, too. But her mother calls and says, 'What do you mean there's no bus?' She calls Karin every morning and tells her different things—like wear a hat because it's cold—things like that. Even though Karin lives with us, her mother acts like her father and I can't take care of her."

Dorothy, 35, New Jersey

"The relationship between me and my husband's ex stinks. We're polite, but we loathe each other. She's patronizing and dogmatic. I tolerate it because I'm raising her only child."

Jerri, 27, Kansas

"She is hostile—even though I have taken the burden of raising her children while she looks out only for herself."

Marcia, 33, Nebraska

Stepfathers rarely have significant contact with their wives' ex-husbands. This is definitely not the case between stepmothers and ex-wives. Twenty-eight percent of the stepmothers in our survey reported handling 50 percent or more of all contacts with their husbands' ex-wives. In many cases, these contacts grow very bitter.

"She even threatened my life!"

Sharon, 41, Idaho

"She falsely believed I starved her son last summer. She cussed me out and threatened to take me to court for child abuse."

Elaine, 40, Washington

She hates me and called me a whore. She is definitely crazy!"

Elizabeth, 43, California

When stepfathers support their stepchildren or adopt them, they rarely expect thanks from the biological father. Stepmothers, on the other hand, often express the feeling that they should receive a "thank you" or some demonstration of gratitude for what they do for the ex-wives' children. This rarely happens. Ex-wives do not say "thank you" to new wives. Step-mothers who expect gratitude, even when they are raising the children, are setting themselves up for disappointment.

The most basic problem is that the ex-wife/new wife relationship is not a relationship of choice—on either side. As ex-wives, we often ask ourselves, "How can I ever make this work with someone as spiteful and insensitive as *she* is?" As remarried wives, we frequently wonder, "How did I ever get into this mess with someone as malicious and cruel as *she* is?"

We did not choose these connections. We are simply linked by one man. Neither one of us really wanted these problems. They were thrust upon us, and now we're told, "For the sake of the children, you have to make the relationship work." What we are not told is *how* to make it work. The truly difficult thing about ex-wife/stepmother problems is that *both* women feel so powerless. In either role, if the "other woman" wants to call us names, she can. If she wants to tell lies about us, she can. If she wants to turn the children against us, she may be able to. In most cases, we truly have very little control over her words or her actions. We can only control our own.

While men seek to gain control through adoption or avoidance, women seek to gain control through words. Sometimes these methods work. Often they do not, and the situation may become so bitter that communication with the ex-spouse is cut off altogether.

CUTTING OFF COMMUNICATION

Many of the remarried men and women in our survey who continued to have difficult relationships with their ex-spouses eventually chose to handle the problem by completely cutting off any verbal contact with the ex-spouse. When children are involved, this is difficult to accomplish, but a surprising number of parents did it anyway.

"I have no contact with him personally. If I have a problem, I go to my attorney and he handles it."

Jean, 48, Iowa

"We have no relationship at all. I don't even talk to her. She is remarried and still wants to be in control—but she is not so I just ignore her."

Josh, 31, Texas

"I only see him at funerals."

Mary, 52, Pennsylvania

"I don't see her often. I *never* speak to her!"

Glen, 33, New Jersey

"I have no relationship with my ex-wife. I have not spoken to her in seven years."

Jack, 32, Texas

For many of our respondents, having no relationship and not speaking was the way in which they handled the scars of divorce. Withdrawal, though, is usually not a good approach to resolving ex-spouse issues. It may *feel* good to the adults involved, but it can harm the children.

EXES WHO ARE FRIENDS

Six percent of our survey respondents reported that they had "very positive" feelings about their ex-spouses. Many of these men and women stressed that their ex-spouses were their "best friends." From our personal perspective, we envied these men and women and admired what they had been able to accomplish. Though they were in the minority, we were especially interested in their comments, hoping that they could shed some light on how to accomplish such positive relationships.

"My ex and I are the best of friends. Our children come first. We have good communication.

Valerie, 39, Texas

"My ex is friendly, caring, and concerned with our two families and our daughter."

Charlene, 46, Tennessee

"We have remained friends and talk often about the kids. We discuss school functions and what's to be bought at Christmas. It's been great for the kids."

Michele, 37, Louisiana

"Even though I have remarried several times, he continues to be supportive and helpful."

Millie, 44, Oklahoma

"My ex was and is my best friend."

Suzanne, 41, Texas

When a man or woman considers an ex-spouse a friend, the new husband or wife nearly always feels friendly toward the former spouse as well. Once again, the remarried couple reacts as a unit. *Together,* they become friends of the ex.

"My husband's ex-wife came and visited for two weeks. She slept with the girls in their room, and Kevin and I slept in the next room. We would wake up and cook breakfast together. She'd cook gravy, and I'd cook eggs. Wendy and Kevin were striving very hard to have a relationship that would be comfortable for the girls so I didn't mind at all."

Samantha, 26, Texas

"She and I are best friends. If my husband and I were to die, I would feel good about her raising our four-year-old son. We think alike."

Sandi, 32, Kansas

"My husband's ex-wife invited us to Christmas dinner, and I just kind of let down and spoke to her as a friend. Then I wrote her a letter saying that I felt a lot of stuff had broken down, and we had a lot of things in common, and I thought I could be her friend, and I just wanted to share that with her. And she wrote back saying she felt the same way, and we became pretty comfortable with each other, and we speak on the phone now, sometimes for a really long time, just networking back and forth."

Karla, 27, New Jersey

A good relationship with an ex-spouse usually depends on how helpful the two families are to each other. When *families* try to work together in raising the children, good relationships become possible.

"My relationship with my husband's ex is improving daily. We are amiable and respect the differences between us. I try to follow through on whatever her decisions on child-rearing are. We are thinking people who put the well-being of the children first."

Beverly, 22, New Jersey

"We used to scream and yell over the phone, but then his ex-wife gave a Tupperware party. My stepdaughter asked me if I would go, and I said, 'Sure. I like Tupperware.' We sat on the couch next to each other and we talked. Then we started talking on the phone about the children. If she had any problems with them, she'd call and talk to me about it. When my stepdaughter got married, I was part of the wedding party and helped the ex-wife with the reception. When we see each other anymore, we hug each other—and we cry together. My husband gets along with my ex very well, too. They sit down and drink together."

Eleanor, 53, Florida

"My ex-husband saw the children almost every day from the time we were separated and through the divorce and all. Now he sees them every weekend in the winter and almost every day in the summertime. The more the children visit, really, the better the situation is in a stepfamily."

Pamela, 25, Delaware

"The more the children visit, really, the better the situation is in a stepfamily." In most stepfamilies, this is true, both for the custodial and the noncustodial parent. When both parents take an active part in their children's lives, it is much easier for everyone—especially the children!

GETTING ALONG WITH "EXES"

Six percent of our survey respondents got along well with exes, but ninety-four percent had problems in this area. Most of those having difficulties communicate with their exes in one of two ways:

1. They give in easily to avoid fighting and then feel resentful.
2. They stand up and fight but end up creating even more anger.

When we use the first method, we turn our anger inward, absorbing it like a sponge. If we use the second method, we may feel better, but our problems frequently will not get solved. Neither of these strategies is effective in promoting successful communication. There is a better way.

In dealing effectively with our "ex" or our partner's "ex," we have two main challenges:

- Deciding *when* to discuss a problem
- Deciding *what* to say when we do discuss a problem

If we and our own spouses can mutually decide beforehand what our guidelines will be, we'll find that it's easier to communicate successfully with ex-husbands and ex-wives. While we cannot control what an ex-spouse says to us, we can, together, decide *whether* we are going to respond and *how* we will respond. It's important to realize that we do not have to respond to an ex. This is often the only decision regarding communication that we can actually control.

If a discussion involves a dispute from the past, it is probably better not to respond. If an argument involves threats or insults, it also is better not to respond. If, however, the communication relates to the children directly, it is usually in their best interests that we do respond. We must do everything in our power, however, to ensure that our communication is effective.

Effective communication between couples and ex-spouses begins by observing seven basic ground rules:

1. Some subjects should not be discussed *at all* with an ex-husband or an ex-wife.
2. Some subjects deserve an *attempt* at discussion.
3. Verbal abuse or threats should not be used.
4. Verbal abuse or threats should not be listened to or reacted to.

5. Requests should be very specific, allowing no room for later misinterpretation.

6. Other people's opinions, comments, or actions regarding the subject under discussion should not be invoked in support.

7. Different options should be considered in arriving at a solution which is in the best interests of the children.

Using these ground rules as a foundation, we personally found it helpful to develop an "Ex-Spouse Communication Chart" for our ex-spouse problems. We planned our strategies beforehand. We anticipated problems and charted our responses. The guidelines let us feel in control. As a result, we tended to be more rational, less emotional and "battle ready."

Everyone's situation is different, but the same subject/problem areas as given in the communication chart arise for most parents and stepparents. Though different couples will make different decisions about what to discuss with exes, what not to discuss, and what to say if a subject is discussed, planning in advance both calms us down and allows us to reinforce our United Front approach to blended family living. We do have some choices, some control.

The "planning in advance" approach illustrated by the communication chart does not eliminate the source of anger between exes. It does not guarantee that our ex or our partner's ex won't do or say hurtful things. It does help us gain more control over the situation and handle communication challenges more productively.

Ex-Spouse Communication Chart

Subject/ Problem Area	Whether or Not to Discuss	What Will We Say?
Our ex wants to discuss travel plans for a child's visit.	It is necessary for us to discuss this.	We will try to be objective and calm. We will stick to the facts. We will make sure we have a firm agreement on times and places.
Our ex is not satisfied with the child support agreement and is threatening to go to court.	It is *not* necessary for us to discuss this.	We will simply state that we have an agreement, that it is fair, and that it is not open for discussion.
Our ex is making derogatory remarks about our current partner.	It is *not* necessary for us to discuss this.	We will simply refuse to discuss or respond to the inflammatory remarks. We may, however, choose to yawn and sound very bored. We will say that if this topic continues, we will hang up.
Our ex wants to discuss a child's health problem.	It is necessary for us to discuss this.	We will attempt to find out what the problem is and what action has been taken. We will offer our views on the subject. We will state our concern and offer whatever level of aid we and our spouse have agreed upon.

We decide what we are willing to discuss—and what we are not willing to discuss. *We* plan our reactions and commentaries beforehand. By doing this, we reduce the likelihood of perpetuating the "war of the exes."

In our own personal situation, with hindsight, we would have handled communication with our exes differently during the early years. There were too many fights, too many accusations from the past, too much anger. The war simply went on too long.

In time, we learned to change our relationships with our exes. We came to realize that, for better or worse, they are part of our extended family. We try not to hurt them, but we also make sure that we do not set ourselves up to be hurt by them. There are many things that we choose not to discuss with them, matters that are irrelevant to the children, issues that would only reopen old wounds. When we do discuss a situation involving one of the children, we stick strictly to facts and logistics. We do not allow explosive issues to erupt.

For us, finally, it became time to reset our course, time to triumph over the scars of the past and turn our energies toward a happier future for everyone. We know that we will never consider our exes our best friends, but we do try our best to promote harmony. We do not criticize them in front of the children. We try to encourage our children to write and visit their other families. We have even begun to urge them to re-establish contact with cousins, aunts, and uncles whom they have not seen for many years because of the divisiveness of divorce. By doing these things, by trying just a bit harder, we create a better environment for those we love—our children.

7

Two Homes For
The Holidays

Children in blended families seldom have to worry about being "home for the holidays." With so much recent focus on the homeless, it is hard to imagine that there are also problems connected to having too many homes, too many obligations.

In our own blended family, most holidays are positive and traditional events since all the children live with us. We celebrate like a nuclear family—barbecues and fireworks on the Fourth of July, new clothes and egg hunts on Easter, turkey and pumpkin pie on Thanksgiving. As parents, we love this arrangement; we do not have to share the children.

But then comes Christmas—what a difference! This is the difficult holiday for us. This is the time of year when Mark and Jilian fly to see their mother, when Brad and Heidi fly to see their father. Christmas means spending hours at crowded airports. We are often there on Christmas Eve or New Year's Eve waiting for planes—dropping children off, picking children up. "'The Night Before Christmas" turns into an evening of reading airline schedule boards.

The house always seems barren and empty after the suitcases are packed, the airport trips are made, and the children are gone. The kids sometimes ask us: "Why can't we be more like the Cosby's?" Christmas is the time of year when we, as parents, wonder: "Why *can't* we be more like the Cosby's?" Other people's families somehow seem so much happier, so much less complicated than ours. We come home from the airport, look at each other, and ask ourselves, "So, what are *we* doing for the holidays?"

We try not even to think about the usual Christmas fantasies—the idyllic Norman Rockwell portrait of mom, dad, and children happily gathered around the tree. One year we went to the home of friends and watched their kids open presents. We didn't enjoy it at all. Our best solution is to leave town. We choose very *un*-Christmasy atmospheres: New Orleans, Galveston Beach, the back roads of Mississippi. For us, getting out of the house works well, and we find ourselves having a good time in decidedly nontraditional ways.

Holidays can be tough for blended families. Our holidays are different from the family specials we all watch on television. There are no Hollywood models for blended families, no television specials idealizing "A Stepfamily Christmas." Television families are not faced with having to share their children with another family.

SHARING KIDS

Sharing kids causes stress—for both families. Either side of the coin—having children arrive or having them leave—is difficult. Many of our survey respondents expressed feelings of loneliness and unhappiness because the children were *not* there for holidays.

"Every Christmas there seems to be a lot of heartache here."
Manuel, 38, Louisiana

"The children stay with their mother. My husband and I had our holidays
with the dog—before he died!"

Charlene, 46, Tennessee

"We do terribly with holidays. I hate them. No matter what we have done
in eleven years, the children always have an excuse for not being with us.
Since my stepson lives in an apartment owned by his mom, and my
stepdaughter lives with her mom, she makes it difficult for them to be
with us."

Elizabeth, 43, California

In other cases, problems arise because the kids *are* there.
The visiting children are more than guests, yet not part of the
"live-in" family. This creates special problems. How should the
children be treated? Should they be entertained since they are,
in some respects, guests? Should they be asked to do chores
since they are, in reality, family members? Parents who only see
their children on vacations, holidays, or weekends are under a
great deal of pressure.

"Holidays are hard because my husband places unfair demands on
my daughter to entertain and be responsible for his son. When his son
comes he plays the 'goody-goody' role to the max around his dad,
and my daughter, who lives with us, looks bad for being honestly herself."

Sandra, 43, South Carolina

"On holidays we see my stepchildren only briefly. The few episodes
we have had when we have all been together have taught us not to
be together any more than we have to."

Gwen, 33, Michigan

Problems frequently erupt for both families due to the inevitable difficulties of shifting children back and forth between

two homes. This is frustrating and can be a catalyst for negative emotional responses. Marilyn's situation is typical of a stepfamily Christmas:

"Christmas is very stressful for all of us. My girls go to their dad's for six to eight hours. The boys, my stepsons, are split two ways. First they go to their mom's and then to my husband's parents. I don't go to my in-laws because I don't get along with them. The girls and I go to my parents after they get back from their dad's, and then we go home and wait for the others. When everyone gets back, and we finally have *our* Christmas, I often feel anger and a sense of betrayal. The kids are also harder to handle in every respect."

Marilyn, 30, Colorado

Many stepparents spend holidays on the road. Trying to keep any kind of Christmas spirit alive when you're caught in the stepfamily shuttle can become an exercise in frustration.

"Mostly, my children have to stay at home alone while my husband and I travel the 600 miles to take his children back to their mom on Christmas Day."

Julia, 45, Wyoming

While Christmas is usually the most emotional holiday for parents and stepparents, other family celebrations are affected as well. In stepfamilies, Thanksgiving can involve much more than just planning a delicious dinner and giving thanks.

"The kids visit their dad for Thanksgiving dinner. We have ours whenever they get home—sometimes at eight or nine at night."

Greg, 37, New Mexico

Many stepchildren have two Thanksgiving dinners, two Halloweens, two birthday parties, two of everything. Like Avis, we remarried adults "try harder." We decorate the house, prepare special foods, and buy expensive gifts. We try to create the perfect Christmas, Thanksgiving, or Hanukkah. Our philosophy often becomes "more is better." The bigger the meal, the better the celebration. The higher the cost, the better the gift. The greater the effort, the greater the love. All this is often doubled for stepchildren.

When it is all over, it becomes very clear that "more is *not* better." The children end up yearning for holidays gone by, idealizing and romanticizing the good old days—before divorce and remarriage changed their lives. In their memories, those holidays were filled with warmth and happiness. It will never be the same again.

There is no way that we can compete with old memories no matter how much we try. The children blame us because things are not the same, and we try to make up for their loss. We try very hard—too hard—and the whole cycle starts all over again. It sometimes takes us years to break this pattern and learn to make the holidays happy and meaningful in new ways.

WHEN CHILDREN VISIT

Visitation, whether it is on holidays, vacations, or weekends, is difficult. The parents who are left at home miss the children. The other parents feel pressured to make the visit a positive one since the children will be there only for a short time. In addition, ex-husbands and ex-wives often have to interact with each other to work out the visitation logistics. All in all, visitation is a tense time for everyone—parents, stepparents, and children.

There are several predictable traps that families fall into when children spend time in two households. Few of us will avoid these traps completely, but we can learn to get out of them a bit more easily.

Power Plays

In nuclear families, parents take the whole concept of home and family for granted. In stepfamilies, children frequently make comments like: "My 'real' home is with Mom" or "I like it best at Dad's." Almost all of us, as parents, fear these comparisons and wonder if the next step will be: "I want to live at Dad's" or "I don't want to visit you anymore."

The automatic tendency to stimulate competition that comes in blended families gives children a great deal of power. Since they did not have the power to "choose" their parents' divorce or their parents' remarriages, they play this, their one clear area of power, to the hilt. As a result, parents sometimes start to feel that nothing they do is good enough, that nothing they have to offer can compare with the other family.

"We always have problems over Easter clothes. One year I made a special effort to go out and buy material and patterns to make my stepdaughter this one particular outfit that she wanted. I'm not that good a seamstress, but I got the material and everything, and I said, 'You need to be sure and come over, so I can fit it to you.' Well, as it turned out, she told her mom that I had bought this stuff, so her mom went out and bought her a dress and what I had done was for nought."

Marian, 44, Kentucky

"My stepchildren are usually with their father on Christmas, and we get them the following day. He has money and buys them everything. I have none and feel inferior at times.

Charles, 34, Ohio

Even if the parents do not feel "inferior," the *opportunity* for competition is always there.

"We have times when the children are together with us as a family and with my husband's family and mine, plus their mother's family and stepfather's family. Christmas ends up being celebrated eight times for my kids."
Jeanne, 26, Ohio

When children celebrate Christmas "eight times," it is inevitable that comparisons will be made. Which grandparent gave them the biggest gift? Where did they have the most fun? Who served the best dinner?

Other holidays and vacations are also problems; they can become a marathon of competition. When two "mothers" are supplying an Easter dress, conflict is inevitable. When one family is financially better off than the other, comparisons also will be made. Sometimes both families begin competing to make the time spent at their house the best time—the most expensive presents, the most fun-filled entertainments, the most excessive displays of loving. Many stepparents complain that their stepchildren are treated as "princes" and "princesses" when they visit.

"When my stepdaughter visits on vacations and holidays, she does everything she can to make my life a an absolute misery. Then I have to explain to my daughter why my husband treats her like she doesn't exist and his daughter like a visiting princess."
Barbara, 24, South Carolina

"Visiting children get the royal treatment, and the live-in children resent it."
Marcella, 38, Virginia

"We get my stepchildren every Christmas for a week. My husband will always give in to his two children out of guilt."
Brie, 27, Alabama

Many parents "give in out of guilt." Parents try to compensate for the pain of divorce and the adjustments of remarriage.

In addition, the myth of the other parent is always present at some level in both households. Children often use this to their advantage. They will portray the other parent as generous and wonderful, and we will try even harder to be viewed as the best parent, the best family.

One stepmother says:

"I resent the 'entertain me, please me' attitude and my husband's inability to say no to his child."
Cherlyn, 28, Tennessee

It's so easy for us to fall into the "entertain me, please me" mode. We want our children to *want* to be with us. We want them to *want* to have fun, but we sometimes end up competing with their other parent. It is hard for us to avoid this since children frequently make comparisons between families. The invitation to competition will always be there, but we need to remind ourselves that we don't have to accept it. We can resist the temptation to prove our popularity in a "best parent" contest.

Household Rules

Whether the children live with us on a permanent basis or visit us for holidays and vacations, we have a right to set the rules and enforce the boundaries within our own home. This is true even if the children visit us for just one day. We do not have to observe the rules and regulations—or lack of rules and regulations—of the other household. We have every right to state our

expectations, needs, and boundaries to the children and to re-
quire that they be met.

The children might not agree. Chances are they will argue
with us about these rules. We will hear charges of "That's not
fair" and "We don't have to do that at Mom's."

"We have rules. Their mother has none. They want her rules in our house."

Kristy, 39, Michigan

"Thank goodness my stepdaughters do not live in my home. They're lazy
when they visit and don't help unless they are told over and over again.
My husband feels that they are visiting, and he wants to do for them."

Charlotte, 38, South Carolina

"At his mother's, my stepson Mike is an only child that is doted upon
and has excessive freedoms for his age. His mother even took him to
go see the movie "Fatal Attraction" when he was ten. Here, at our
home, we have had three babies in five years. Our household is more
chaotic, and we have to make every effort to maintain some form of
sanity. We have to have some house rules and expect each child to
exhibit a sense of responsibility—picking up, cleaning up after
themselves—just some simple chores and duties, but Mike's mother told
him that he 'doesn't have to take any crap off of me'."

JoAnne, 37, Indiana

It is difficult for children to switch households; they are not
chameleons. At the same time, they must learn to adapt to the
fact of change. All through their lives, they will be asked to adapt
to different people and different places, and it truly will not hurt
them to get some early practice.

We also need to make the rules and standards for our home
clear. If the other household has different values, we do not need
to worry about them. The two sets of standards do not have to

blend. The only blending we need to be concerned about is the blending that takes place in our own home—when the children are with us.

Giving Too Much

Stepmothers, especially, report that holidays and visitation take a strong emotional toll. Women are programmed to glamorize holidays and visits and to feel responsible for "making them happen"—the perfect presents, the perfect dinner, the perfect family. The only problem is that everything usually doesn't turn out perfectly, and the martyred mother feeling is lurking in the shadows. "No one else around here cares about the dinner/the house/the dirty clothes/the messy rooms/*or how hard I work!*" Stepmothers begin to feel like maids and housekeepers, someone whose feelings do not really matter.

"I'm usually treated like a maid and babysitter when the stepchildren visit. I'm the 'bad guy' while my husband is the ideal weekend father.
Kristy, 39, Michigan

"I feel like a slave to his children while they are here."
Candace, 38, Ohio

"We entertain the visiting children more because they are here less often. I feel unwanted and hated. My stepchildren do not see me as an authority figure who has rights in the household. There is special competition between my stepdaughter and me when she visits on how the household will be run and arranged."
Helen, 41, Tennessee

Children do not visit to satisfy our needs; they are there to satisfy their own. But we have needs, too; we're not there solely to satisfy the children's needs. We have to recognize that we can't do it all. Everything does not have to be perfect and, most likely, everything will not be perfect.

For fathers and stepfathers, holidays and visitation put finances right on the line. Expectations, guilt, and financial burdens can combine to build a strong case of resentment. When there are complaints by stepfathers, it is almost always in this realm.

"We ignore holidays unless a gift is required. And then we don't even get a 'Thank you' but a 'Is that all?'"
David, 44, Tennessee

Financial sacrifice can be just as frustrating as giving time and emotional energy. There is a real danger in overgiving. Stepchildren frequently do not say "thank you" to stepparents, and, if large sacrifices have been made, this can lead to hurt feelings. It helps to recognize this fact in advance. We must realize that we have choices. We do not have to feel overwhelmed and then feel "used" when we're not appreciated.

Traditions

A popular catch phrase for stepparents in the 1990's is: "Create your own traditions." Over time, it does become much easier for us to build our own traditions. At first, though, this can be quite difficult. The past is still far too vivid. There are a lot of "shoulds" in everybody's lives, and there is also a great deal of leftover emotion, much of it focused on holidays.

Food, especially, can become a battleground. Should it be ham, turkey, or rack of lamb? Should it be matzos, enchiladas, or hot dogs? Ritual suddenly becomes very important. When should the Christmas presents be opened? How should the New Year be celebrated? Perhaps these choices don't seem worth fighting over, but behind each argument there is a symbol, an emotional investment. For children, resisting new ideas is a way of preserving the past. For them, which family's tradition will be observed becomes a symbolic struggle.

Many stepfamilies have handled this kind of problem by blending traditions: turkey *and* ham, potato kugel *and* candied yams, Christmas Eve presents *and* Christmas Day presents. This is probably the easiest way to resolve the conflicts. Good feelings are more important than rigidity in the face of my tradition/your tradition arguments.

It is also possible to combine old traditions and new options. We can compromise without clashing with the past. Along with the old, we can introduce an event, a ritual, or a food that is completely new to everyone. When old traditions are not ignored, children are open to new ones, and soon these additions will turn into "our" family's traditions.

COPING STRATEGIES

Whenever we share kids with another parent, there are going to be challenges to rules and boundaries. This is especially true for the parents with children who are coming to visit.

We asked our respondents to comment on how "visiting" children are treated versus how "live-in" children are treated in their homes. The comparison was clear: 39% of visiting children got more adult attention, 46% did fewer chores, 38% had fewer rules, and 44% were punished less often than children living in the home. This pattern clearly illustrates the fact that visitation creates the potential for resentment—both for adults and the live-in children.

A Short Quiz

Faced with these problems, what is the *single* most important thing we can do to ensure happy visits for our stepchildren? Is the answer:

(a) Giving the children lots of hugging and affection?
(b) Keeping them busy and planning entertainment that they'll enjoy?
(c) Buying them special presents to show we care?
(d) Cooking their favorite dinners and having "kid pleasing" snacks on hand?
(e) Planning the visit so that we, too, will enjoy it?

All of the above are positive things that we can do for visiting children. Yet the best thing we can do is answer (e): Planning the visit so that we, too, will enjoy it. There is a strong correlation between *our* enjoyment of the children's visit and *their* enjoyment of the time spent with us.

Many remarried couples explain that, when the children visit, they try to provide "quality" time to make the children happy. The concept of quality time is a good one, but too often it is interpreted as doing anything and everything the children want to do. If the kids want to eat at McDonald's, *we* eat at McDonald's. If they want to go to two movies in one day, *we* go to two movies. We want them to be HAPPY. Unfortunately, they often end up as exhausted and as sick of junk food as we do.

More significantly, they tend to develop an "entertain me, please me" attitude. If we allow this to happen, the children become more egocentric. They care less and less about what other people want. They expect to be catered to in *both* of their homes, and they end up as very self-centered adults. This is why it is so important for us to set limits for visiting children and stepchildren.

Setting Limits

One of the main problems we face with our children is manipulative verbal interactions. When children or stepchildren try to get something extra from us—and they *will* try—our natural inclination is to try to buy the child's goodwill by giving in. A typical visiting child scenario would go like this:

Visiting Child: Dad, I don't have anything to wear. All the other kids at school dress better than I do. I *really* need some clothes.

Dad: What does your mother do with her child support? That's supposed to go for your clothes.

Child: I can't ask her. She has a tough time making it. Her car broke down, there's the insurance, the doctor bills, and everything else.

Dad: But we have those problems here, too.

Child: So is it my fault? I didn't tell you to get divorced and make my life miserable.

Dad: You know I don't try to make your life miserable. What happened to the $300 Christmas check?

Child: My stereo broke and I had to get a new one. Just forget it. Forget about the clothes. I'm sorry I brought it up. I'm sorry I even came to visit since I'm such a burden to you.

Dad: Come on. You're not a burden. How much do you need?

This is a familiar scene in stepfamilies. The visiting child complains and makes Dad feel guilty. Dad resists but then gives in. Later, Dad's new wife protests, and another familiar scene begins.

Stepmother:	I can't believe you did that. Another $200 after the $300 we just gave her?
Dad:	I told you the Christmas money had to go for a new stereo.
Stepmother:	What about the $700 a month her mother gets for child support? Isn't that supposed to cover clothes?
Dad:	You know I can't control where the child support goes. The kid needs clothes.
Stepmother:	My kids need clothes, too, and now we'll barely have enough to eat on for the rest of the month. I can't believe you gave her that $200. I won't stand for it!

In blended families, giving in to the demands of one person often means that another person is going to end up being angry or disappointed. It is virtually impossible to please everyone. Once again, the most effective approach is for a husband and a wife to form a United Front, to make decisions together—and enforce them.

When our children visit, we want the visit to be happy, especially for them. If it isn't, it makes us feel guilty and affects our self-esteem as parents. This is why those of us with visiting children have ongoing problems in setting limits. Even when we do set them, it's hard to follow through because we don't want to alienate the kids during our limited time with them.

The reality, though, is that when any of us live with another person, even for a short period of time, there's no escaping the necessity for establishing some limits and turning down some requests. Setting limits means being honest in relationships. It's telling the other person how we feel and drawing the line when a request is not acceptable. As parents and stepparents, we only have so much time and money, and sometimes we have to deny requests—even if we feel guilty about it.

Verbal Self-Defense

When children come to visit, parents and stepparents often feel that they're under scrutiny. Sometimes they are. Children don't hesitate to test the waters. Parents need to be realistic about this and expect it. Parents also need to plan their strategies to cope with it.

This can be a very real challenge. The temptation is to counterattack, to reply to the blamer with blame.

Visiting Child: At Dad's, we eat out all the time. That's more fun.
Mother: It's mean of you to keep telling me how great things are at Dad's. I'm sick of hearing about it.

Another temptation is to answer with a question.

Visiting Child: At Dad's, we eat out all the time. That's more fun.
Mother: Why is that more fun? Why is restaurant food better than my home cooking?

Neither approach is effective. In the first, everyone becomes defensive. In the second, the child will probably tell you, in no uncertain terms, *why* it's more fun to eat out all the time.

The best approach is to respond to a negative comment with a positive response. Do not place blame. Do not ask a question. Instead:

1. Acknowledge the child's comment and feelings.
2. Clearly state your feelings and your intent.

In all likelihood, this will quickly stop the confrontation or complaint. At the same time, the response is so positive that the child will not feel threatened or defensive.

Following are some examples of positive responses to negative comments in typical family situations.

Positive Responses To Negative Comments

Child's Comment	Parent's Response
At Dad's, we eat out all the time. That's more fun.	I'm glad that it's fun for you at your Dad's, but it's important to us that we have *family* meals at home when you're here.
We stay up as late as we want at "home."	That's okay when you're there, but when you're here we want you to get plenty of rest so you'll be able to enjoy the things we do together.
I hate you and I always will. Stepmothers are mean.	Oh, I think you'll change your mind after you get to know me better. I'm really a pretty neat person.
Is that all I get? Dad spent $500 on me for Christmas.	We wish we could spend that much, but we can't. We don't feel money is the most important thing. The time we spend together is.
He's not my dad, and I'll never call him "Dad."	That's true; he isn't your dad and he isn't trying to take your dad's place. If you give him a chance, though, I think you'll learn that he can be your friend.
My mom's a better cook than you are. She never makes eggplant.	I'm glad that you enjoy her food. I'm pleased that you're eating the eggplant, too, because it's important that you try different things. Who knows? Someday you might try something you like.
We have to go camping on our vacation again? Dad takes us to neat places like Disneyland.	You're a lucky kid. With two families, you get to have all sorts of different experiences.

This type of mental reprogramming isn't easy to carry out on a day-to-day basis. It is, however, quite effective once we learn to use it. Large changes usually come more easily after a series of small successes.

ENJOYING VISITING CHILDREN

We all want to enjoy our children when they visit and help them enjoy themselves as well. Beneath their sometimes difficult facades, children want visits that are happy and meaningful just as much as we do. Yet we often attempt to achieve this common goal in all the wrong ways.

When children visit, they should not be put on a pedestal or treated like visiting royalty. They should, instead, be made a part of the family routine, whether they are there for one day or six months. Although the children may be consulted, it is the husband and wife who should plan the activities for the weekend, vacation, or holiday.

The children are there to visit us and be a part of our lives, and we have a right to do the things that we want to do, too. We need to clearly establish, in our own minds, what we will do during the visit and what we will not do.

Most importantly, we must remember that it is the marriage that should be on center stage, not the children. If our marriage is healthy, if our home is happy, *all* of the individuals who are a part of it—and who visit it—will be nurtured by that strong, secure foundation of love.

As stepfamilies become the most common type of family in America, two homes for the holidays will also become the norm. It will not always be easy, but we, as parents, can make it work.

8

The Extended Family: In-laws, Ex-Laws, and Out-Laws

Julia was twenty when she married James. She had already been married and divorced once and had a one-year-old daughter, Casey. James was twenty-five and widowed, with a two-year-old son, Tommy.

Julia and James' marriage was very successful, and Casey and Tommy grew up as sister and brother. The blended family was close, and the children adapted well to their new parents. The people who did *not* adapt as well were James' parents and Julia's parents. Somehow, they could not view the new family and children as a "real" family.

"James' parents are polite, but my daughter Casey is not 'family.' She is not even introduced as such. My own parents know that I love my stepson Tommy as my own, and I insist that he be treated well, but he is still not the same to them as Casey, their granddaughter."

Julia, 39, Tennessee

In contrast to James' parents and Julia's parents were the parents of James' *first* wife. Since his first wife (Tommy's mother) had tragically died in an accident, these grandparents were delighted that their grandson had a new family and instantly embraced Julia as "family."

"My husband's first wife's family has been so good to me. They treat me like a family member—and they call my daughter 'Tommy's sister.' We visit them a lot and spend holidays with them."

Julia, 39, Tennessee

WHAT IS A FAMILY?

To Julia and James, the meaning of the word "family" took on new connotations. Many of our survey respondents, like Julia and James, felt that the definition of family goes beyond blood ties and in-law connections. We instinctively know when we belong, when we are a part of a family; we also know when we are not!

Webster's has twenty-two definitions of the term "family," but none of these explanations truly captures the essence of a word that is so important to all of us who have divorced and remarried. Neither does the official Bureau of the Census definition come close to what a family really is in the 1990's. As blended families become more common than the so-called traditional families, we have to start redefining our terms in concepts that go far beyond the worlds of "Ozzie and Harriet" and "Leave It to Beaver." Stepfamilies link people together in unusual ways. In the 1990's, our family trees, with stepkin and ex-in-laws, are sprouting unique new branches.

Our personal family tree—and the changes it has gone through over the years—is but one example.

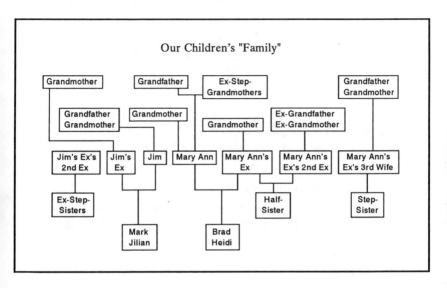

Our Children's "Family"

As you can see, our children now have "family" relationships that carry labels such as ex-stepfather, ex-stepmother, ex-step-grandmother, and ex-stepsister, and our diagram doesn't even attempt to depict step-relatives such as stepuncle, stepaunt by marriage, or step-first-cousin. All of these relationships are quite real, and they have affected our lives in ways that we never could have imagined when we were living in nuclear families.

While our family tree is a somewhat confusing tangle of family and ex-family "kin," it is not unusually complicated as stepfamilies go. And, despite its web of complexities, we feel that it has some positive aspects. Most importantly, our children have had the opportunity to form new relationships across racial and cultural lines as a part of their extended family experiences. Brad and Heidi have an aunt who is Korean and an uncle who is African-American. Mark and Jilian have an aunt who is Japanese. There are Hispanic, European, and Chinese cousins. They are all a part of our extended blended family, and in this there is a strong hope for the future. Human beings are coming together in a much more universal sense that ever before.

Grandparents abound within our family. One is a carpenter. Another is a retired teacher. Still another is a realtor. At times this abundance of relatives becomes overwhelming; more often it seems somewhat humorous. On the whole, the "positives" far outweigh the "negatives."

In a very real sense, blended families today are reinventing the whole meaning of the word family, and, as this occurs, human understanding is growing as well. "Family" is becoming more a feeling than a word that we try to define.

In the presence of so many complex and ambiguous relationships, the potential for problems is inevitable. And while aunts, uncles, and cousins are usually not that significant in "making or breaking" the new stepfamily, grandparents do wield significant power.

STEPGRANDPARENTS

Stepgrandparents are much more important in the blended family system than they—or we—may realize. The choices that they make will have an impact on many people: their own children, their children's spouses, their grandchildren, and their stepgrandchildren. With so many children affected by divorce and remarriage and so many parents facing the problems of blending two families together, grandparents have a choice: they can add fuel to the already existing fires, or they can offer us that additional bit of love and support which might help our new family make it through.

In many ways, it is difficult for *step*grandparents to define what they should do in regard to their *step*grandchildren. How should they relate to them? Our "ex" in-laws, our children's biological grandparents, also have difficulties in relating to us, their former daughters-in-law and sons-in-law, and must learn to redefine their role in our lives as well as in the lives of their grandchildren.

Our survey respondents tended to place grandparents in two categories: those who accept the new spouse and stepchildren as "family" and those who do *not*.

TWO STYLES OF GRANDPARENTING

When Wendy, 24, married Bill, 30, they each brought two children to the marriage. Wendy had full custody of her two sons, and Bill had joint custody of his daughters. Bill's daughters always lived with the family from Friday until Wednesday of each week but sometimes came a day earlier or stayed a day later. For Wendy, Bill, and their children, this arrangement worked well.

The main problem in the marriage was Wendy's parents. They accepted Bill as Wendy's husband but did not accept Karen and Sally as part of their family. Even after seven years, the difficulties persisted.

"They never really want to have Karen and Sally over at all. For example, my parents will call up and say, 'Why don't you come over for dinner?' and I'll say, 'Well, we have Karen and Sally over.' So they'll say, 'Oh well. Maybe another time.' It would have been a lot easier for me these seven years if I would have felt freer to come and go and see them when I wanted and have them over. They don't even want to talk with me about the problems or about the girls. I think that they missed out. When the kids get older they're going to realize that they blew it. Karen and Sally don't even know what to call them."

Wendy

In contrast to Wendy's parents, Bill's parents handled the situation much differently. They opened up their hearts and homes to Wendy's sons and accepted them as their grandchildren.

"His parents have accepted my children totally and give equal gifts to all four children and spend equal time with all of them. My boys call their stepfather's parents Grandpa and Grandma."

Wendy, 30, Oregon

Wendy's parents, like so many others, found the remarriage of their daughter difficult to cope with. They had no desire for "instant grandchildren." As a result, they withdrew from Wendy when her stepchildren were at her home. A large number of our respondents reported similar situations.

"My widowed mother really tries. She sends Christmas gifts and cash in birthday cards to my husband's children. His parents, though, don't send anything to mine. They don't even know when their birthdays are since they've never asked. They are not real well off financially, but they could at least send cards."

Jean, 48, Iowa

"In the nine years I've been married, my parents have only seen my stepdaughter once and have very little interest in her."

Katherine, 40, New York

"My spouse's parents do not wish to have anything to do with me, my son, or my daughter."

Annette, 32, New Jersey

When grandparents withdraw from relationships with their stepgrandchildren or do not fully acknowledge them, problems are created for the entire blended family. Both the parents and stepparents resent it, and the stepchildren are hurt most of all.

Children seldom find it strange to gain another set of grandparents but, rather, are usually open and responsive to—and definitely in need of—any extra love and attention they can get. They find it hard to understand when their stepgrandparents do not respond to them.

Though it is sometimes hard for grandparents to embrace new children as part of the family, if they can do so, they will be building bridges to the new family rather than constructing walls around it. To stepmothers, especially, grandparental support and acceptance of *all* the children is very important.

"The grandparents have all been wonderfully and totally accepting. To them, it just means more grandchildren!"
Kimberly, 45, Colorado

"My husband's mother treats my children the same as her biological grandchildren."
Monica, 43, Texas

"All four grandparents have opened their hearts to the children. Each one always receives the same amount from the grandparents."
Kathy, 25, California

GRANDPARENT PROBLEM AREAS

Societal stepfamily guidelines are blurry at best. Many grandparents simply do not know how to react or relate to their stepgrandchildren. For them, this is a new and strange situation. They have their own set of fears, their own set of concerns. Do they owe these other children anything? Is there enough money to go around? What about the question of family inheritance? Is it possible to ever feel the same about someone else's children? Aren't blood ties stronger than other ties? And, the question that concerns them most: will their own grandchildren feel left out or jealous?

In reality, there are no rules. Yet there *are* guidelines, ways that grandparents can deal with sensitive areas of stepfamily living and help the new family succeed in building a happy life together. The three most important areas regarding grandparents that our survey respondents mentioned again and again were:

1. Grandparents should treat *all* of the children equally in terms of gifts.
2. Grandparents should view themselves as part of the stepchildren's family.
3. Grandparents should include *all* of the children in family gatherings.

Gift Giving

For children, one of the most important symbols of equal treatment by grandparents is gifts or remembrances. Stepparents often "rate" their spouse's parents' performance in this way as well. Over and over again, our survey respondents viewed gifts as tangible evidence of caring.

"My mother loves to buy things for my stepdaughters."
Jack, 32, Texas

"My parents, after more than six years, are finally giving my stepchildren Christmas presents."
Wendy, 30, Oregon

"My parents always give my stepdaughter birthday and Hanukkah presents, hugs and kisses, etc."
Jodie, 31, Minnesota

None of our survey respondents expected grandparents to lavish gifts and money on stepgrandchildren. They were, however, very sensitive about fairness, about equal treatment. Parents and stepparents alike felt that grandparents should treat all the children in the family equally, that biological grandchildren should not receive more than stepgrandchildren.

"My husband's parents give presents equally and try their best to be equal."
Irene, 33, Louisiana

For many grandparents, equal treatment is difficult. They feel that the stepgrandchildren are *not* their grandchildren and that, in the absence of actual bloodlines, they do not have the same obligation to them.

"My mother-in-law is friendly and courteous to my children, but they are not accepted in the same way as her natural grandchild. For example: graduation gifts. The natural grandchild got $500 and my son got $20. Actions are notably different."
Fran, 43, Virginia

Not a single stepparent in our survey characterized a grandparent as cruel, but they did, nonetheless, find unequal treatment hurtful. Most grandparents do not realize the impact of their actions and words. They also do not realize how much power they truly have in helping the new blended family to succeed.

Overall, 55 percent of our survey respondents felt that their new mothers- and fathers-in-law had usually treated their biological grandchildren and stepgrandchildren equally. More importantly, in "successful" blended families, 67 percent of these stepgrandparents were reported as having treated the grandchildren equally.

> In 67% of Successful Remarriages:
> Grandparents Treat All of the Children Equally

In stepfamilies with ongoing problems, only 33 percent of stepgrandparents were perceived as being "fair" in their treatment of their grandchildren.

Family Relationships

The role of grandparents is an important variable in stepfamily happiness, and families whose grandparents had helped were enthusiastic in expressing their gratitude and good feelings. Little things often mean a great deal to adults who are coping with the already difficult process of blending.

"Jack's mother was so proud of the family picture we had made of Jack, me, and my girls. She said, 'Now I've got pictures of grandkids to show off.' As far as my relationship with them and their relationship with my children—it's just too good to be true!"

Shana, 31, Texas

"My folks consider the stepkids their grandchildren. The boys call them 'Grandpa' and 'Grandma.'"

Carol Ann, 32, California

"My parents love my husband and count his kids among their grandchildren. My husband's grandfather is still alive and counts my kids as his greatgrandchildren."

Marilyn, 40, Pennsylvania

Once again, "family" comes down to "feeling." For parents and stepparents alike, it can be very helpful if grandparents view themselves as grandparents—to *all* of the children.

Family Gatherings

Ninety-nine percent of the time parents will be hurt if all the children are not included in family gatherings. When the children are there, they should also be introduced as members of the family and fully accepted as such. It can be quite difficult for the new family's togetherness if they are not.

"My wife's children are not made to feel a 'real' part of the family. Getting together for the holidays is a nice but very shallow experience."
Karl, 46, Pennsylvania

"My husband's father always reminded my children that they were only *step*-grandchildren."
Joanna, 48, Virginia

The situation is always much happier when grandparents can fully accept everyone.

"My parents accepted the stepchildren, and they always treated them as natural grandchildren at family gatherings and financially as well."
Phyllis, 62, Iowa

"Neither set of parents (mine or his) has ever even used the word 'step.'"
Jerri, 27, Kansas

For grandparents, who have been married for most of their lives to each other, the divorce-extended families of their children pose complications. This uncharted territory is difficult to travel. In the melange of relatives, ex-relatives, and new relatives by marriage, even the most simple activities become fraught with confusion. Etiquette has not kept pace with the new challenges created by blended families. Grandparents frequently do not know how to handle stepfamily situations.

What is proper? How should they introduce their new "instant grandchildren?" How do the new grandchildren view them?

The Chinese have an elaborate system for defining different relatives. The relationships are immediately apparent. For example, they have seven words to distinguish the word aunt, differentiating between a mother's older and younger sister, a father's sister, and the wife of a mother's brother.[1] Our vocabulary is much looser and has not kept up with our rapidly changing life styles.

Grandparents can refer to their new grandchildren as our stepgrandchildren, our daughter-in-law's (or son-in-law's) children, or our grandchildren. It might seem awkward at first to simply say "our grandchildren," but the families who are able to do this usually have the closest relationships. By doing this, they are showing the grandchildren that they value them *all.*

In our own personal situation, we have been fortunate in the extended family area. Our parents and siblings instinctively knew that it would make blending easier for us if all the children were treated as equally as possible. Birthday, Christmas, and graduation gifts have always been equal. Family gatherings automatically include all four children. Most importantly, they are all considered grandchildren—and nieces and nephews—and the word "step" has never been used by them.

When grandparents do not understand the complexities of this situation, it is up to us, as parents and stepparents, to let them know what part we would like them to play in our lives and the lives of our children. If they can come to see their roles as opportunities to help children who are not "family" by birth, the rewards will be high for everyone. By welcoming all the children as "our children," they will be helping us greatly in building our new families.

THE PARENTS OF "EXES": IN-LAWS OR OUT-LAWS?

For those of us who are divorced, the most sensitive area of all in coping with extended family life is in knowing how to relate to our ex-husband or ex-wife's family. Usually, we no longer consider them *our* family. Yet they are still *our children's family*.

This is such an unnatural reversal in roles that few of us can escape some feelings of being left out. We used to attend all the family reunions, weddings, funerals, Bar Mitzvahs, and graduations, and now, suddenly, we are no longer "family." Overnight, we have gone from valued family member to *persona non grata*. For those of us who were close to our former family, this can be painful. The situation is further accentuated whenever our children are included in an important gathering and we are clearly excluded.

HOW SHOULD WE DEAL WITH THE "FORMER" FAMILY?

Three-fourths of our survey respondents felt that it was important for children to stay in touch with their "other family" even if concessions had to be made. Often these concessions were difficult, but usually they turned out to be worth the effort.

When Lauren, 20, married Tom, 26, she loved Tom's three-year-old son Brad and he returned her affection.

"Wherever I went I had this little three year old tagging along and we'd go all sorts of places and he'd always say 'Oh, I love you!'"

Lauren

Unfortunately, Brad's grandmother was upset when he told her about his love for his stepmother.

"Brad's grandmother, his mother's mother, actually told Brad that he couldn't love me. All of a sudden one day, we were driving around and he said, 'I love you, Daddy.' Then he looked at me and said, 'But I don't love you. I like you, but I don't love you.' All of a sudden this three-year-old had had a change of heart. Instead of getting upset, I tried to accept his feelings. He told me that his grandmother said he could love his mom and love his dad, but I was somebody else and I shouldn't be loved. I tried to tell him that it was okay to love everybody, but somehow it wasn't enough to satisfy him."

Lauren

Lauren realized that the only person who could really change Brad's mind was his grandmother, and, instead of being angry, Lauren tried to be understanding, to make concessions.

"We went to drop him off at his grandparents' house, and his mother was there and his grandmother was there and he came running to me to ask permission for something. I told him, 'You've got to check with your mom 'cause she's in charge. We're not in my house anymore.' After that, I had absolutely no problems with the grandmother. I think that she was afraid I was going to try to come between Brad and his mom, and when she saw that I respected his mother, she respected me."

Lauren, 27, Pennsylvania

Lauren had never known Brad's "other grandmother" well, but she most certainly did not want to come between her stepson and his grandmother. And, like so many of our respondents, she felt that the compromise she offered was well worth the effort that it took on her part.

Cheryl, then 28, had a different situation. She had always been close to her ex-husband's mother and was hurt when her ex-mother-in-law blamed her for the divorce.

"My ex-husband was a teacher, and he started running around with one of his students. I finally just kicked him out and said enough of this. I can tolerate a lot, but I couldn't tolerate that. Even with this problem, his parents, you know, said right away: 'What did you do, Cheryl, to cause this?' They had such a blind spot for their only child."

Cheryl

Even though emotions were raw during the divorce, Cheryl wanted to maintain a good relationship with her ex-in-laws, the grandparents of her children. She succeeded to a much greater extent than she ever believed would be possible.

"To this day, they come here and visit my new husband and me. They even bring Christmas presents for my second husband and for my child from this marriage."

Cheryl, 37, South Dakota

Surprisingly, Lauren and Cheryl were typical of many of our respondents. They were parents and stepparents who tried to maintain ties and a good relationship with the former family.

Family relationships can often be maintained after divorce, and, for the sake of the children, it is usually worth the effort it takes to make it happen. Family boundaries do not have to be strictly redrawn following a divorce and remarriage. When a family member dies and a spouse remarries, the former spouse is usually still seen as family. Why is divorce so much more *final* than death when it comes to cutoffs and exclusions of former family members?

Our children need stable family relationships. To help achieve this, we need to work actively to ensure that they do not get cut off from their "other grandparents." This is usually not all that difficult to accomplish. In nine cases out of ten, even under initially trying circumstances, we will find—as Cheryl did—that our former in-laws are surprisingly receptive. They do not want to be cut off from the children any more than the children want to be cut off from them. In our own stepfamily, we have always urged—and reminded!—our children to remember their "other grandparents" (the parents of our ex-spouses) on birthdays and other important occasions.

If, through a little effort and compromise, we can keep that important relationship alive, it is effort well spent. Grandparents should not have to pay the price for the divorces of their children.

A FAMILY IS WHAT WE MAKE IT

In America in the 1990's, there will be more blended families than traditional families. This will have an impact on all of us as we redefine in our own ways what a family truly is.

Many of us will simply rewrite the rules. Instead of categorizing kin according to bloodlines, we will think of family as those people whom we can count on. We will see less emphasis put on "blood" relationships and more placed on "connecting" relationships. We will know a family when we see one—in a way that goes beyond a mother, father, and their kids. Families will consist of men, women, and children who love and care for each other. Families will offer support, sustenance, and substance. We will not simply recreate a new version of the nuclear family. Instead, we will be a part of a network of family-like relationships that offer their own rewards.

As men and women, we will continue both to join together and to separate from one another; we will continue to marry, divorce, and remarry. Yet, for the children, the essence of "the family" will remain. For the sake of our children, we will work to strengthen new family ties—but not by breaking the old connections at the same time. Children need both—the new and the old.

Our children have much to gain by this network of family relationships and interconnections. Although many of the members of our redefined families will not live under the same roof, they will still contribute to the security and growth of one another. In-laws, ex-laws, and step-in-laws will not be seen as *out*-laws but, rather, as a valuable part of a larger family constellation—a blended kinship.

Divorce and remarriage are facts of life. They will continue to affect us all. Stepfamilies create long chains of interwoven relationships. Some are good, and some are bad. Yet they are all, in some way, lessons in living to us and to our children. They are a part of what we are and what we wish to become. Families name us and help define us. If we can value them from that perspective and treat them as an opportunity for growth, our children will benefit greatly.

As "family," we all need each other.

LIVING HAPPILY IN THE NEW AMERICAN FAMILY

For those of us who have survived the first few years, stepfamily life becomes easier. We have gone through the "aftershock" reverberations. We now know what we got ourselves into. We know what we can realistically expect—and what we cannot. Through trial and error, we have learned how to coexist with ex-husbands and ex-wives. We have redefined our family and have made our own peace with the past. We have also discovered that the phrase "united we stand" has a special meaning for us in dealing with our children.

Successful blending, though, is about more than simply surviving. It's about living and loving and, as the final part of this book suggests, "happily-ever-aftering." *The New American Family* can be a family in which there is a mutual caring about the growth of each individual, a source of strength, a place of connection. This is what we all strive for. "Blending," at its best, is really "loving."

Part Three

Living Happily
Ever After

9

Structured Discipline Communication: Helping Your Child Succeed

Virtually all of us who marry for a second time yearn for a "happily-ever-after." Happily-ever-after endings do not come easily to blended families, but they are indeed possible.

When we began writing *The New American Family,* we had children living at home. Three years later, life is much different. The "kids" are all in college now. A chapter of our lives is completed.

In retrospect, we feel that the most important thing we were able to do for our children was to help them move out of our lives and get started with their own. After nine years of blended family living, they are no longer dependent on us. As we watch them reach out toward life, we feel that we, too, have succeeded— by helping them to move on.

In many ways, living in a blended family forced our children to grow up. They got "hands-on" experience in dealing with new relationships and in working through problems. Our family had its difficulties as we first began to live together, but, over time, we did learn that most problems have solutions. We also learned that in blended families you have to share—and to care.

THE CRUCIAL FIRST FIVE YEARS

Our stepfamily survived the first five years. After that, things began to get easier. Our children not only adapted to the stepfamily, but they also learned to flourish as they faced other changes in their lives. Adjusting to college life was no problem. Going out into the working world for the first time was also unusually easy. We feel that, ultimately, children benefit by blended family living—even with its problems. During those crucial first five years, few of us believe that this is possible.

For the adults in blended families, surviving the first five years usually means surviving the children. Most first marriages break up *after* five years. Most second and third marriages break up *before* the five year mark. The variable is, of course, the children. In first marriages, couples try to stay together for the sake of the children, children who live with both of their biological parents. In stepfamilies, two-thirds of the marriages which break up do so because of conflicts with children, conflicts between children and their stepparents. If we can get over the "kid hurdle," we can make our marriages work.

In our survey, we found a strong correlation between successful marriages and positive stepchild relationships. We also found that problems in marriage were usually intertwined with problems with stepchildren.

We asked our respondents the following questions:

- After marriage, did you find it easy or difficult to relate to your stepchildren?
- Have your stepchildren treated you better or worse since your marriage than before?
- How satisfied are you with the relationships you have established with your stepchildren?

The responses to these questions were:

- Eighty-nine percent of the men and women who were having marital difficulties stated that it was not easy to relate to stepchildren.
- Fifty-nine percent of these same respondents felt that their stepchildren treated them worse *after* marriage than *before* marriage.
- Eighty-one percent answered that they were *not* satisfied with their relationships with their stepchildren.

A direct correlation clearly exists between marital problems in blended families and negative relationships between the step-parents and stepchildren.

Those marriages which succeed show the same type of pattern. Just as marital problems and negative stepparent/stepchild relationships go together, so do happy marriages and positive stepparent/stepchild relationships. In stepfamilies, we must redefine the parenting role as we face very different circumstances. Most of us quickly discover that we have to be active, not passive, parents. Nonparticipation does not work; positive discipline does.

DISCIPLINING STEPCHILDREN

The word "discipline" is often associated with the word "punishment," giving it negative connotations. In reality, discipline does not mean punishment. *Webster's New Twentieth Century Dictionary* says that discipline is a "branch of knowledge or learning" and "a training that develops self-control, character, orderliness, and efficiency." The word discipline comes from the Latin word "disciple" which means "learner."

This is the way we perceive discipline. We view it as providing structure in our children's lives and teaching them the principles of success. We feel that it is important for us to set appropriate limits for our children so that they can learn to live successfully in today's complex, competitive society.

In blended families, stepparents often rationalize their discomfort with setting limits for their stepchildren. They tell themselves, "These are not *my* children."

Biological parents also find disciplining children uncomfortable. Instead of setting appropriate boundaries, they say, "These kids have gone through the pain of divorce and the adjustment of remarriage. It's been hard enough for them already."

Divorce is inevitably hard for children, but this does not mean that we should be more indulgent and permissive in order to make things "easy" for them. If we do this, we can end up hurting them rather than helping them. In essence, by making things easy, we "de-skill" our children for living. When it's time for them to leave home and stand on their own two feet, they do not have the appropriate living skills, confidence, or abilities to be successful. Life then becomes much harder—not easier.

For a blended family to succeed, discipline must be a part of family living. Children should be expected to contribute meaningfully to the family. They should be expected to accept responsibility for their own actions and words and to treat family members with respect.

We asked our respondents the question: "Do you find it difficult or easy to discipline your stepchildren?" In families with ongoing problems, seventy-one percent of stepparents answered "Difficult." Many parents and stepparents found disciplining difficult at first but then came to realize how important it truly is.

When Beverly first married, she felt that she couldn't say anything to her stepchildren about their behavior. They were not *her* children.

"At first I thought, 'I can't really say anything to them. They're not my children.' But it got worse and worse—and it began to affect my own children. After my stepchildren visited, my children started running around trying to punch me and shoot toy guns at me and stuff like that. It was like, 'Who are these monsters?' My stepsons were doing things I wouldn't allow my own children to do—things that I could never condone like name-calling and pushing the other kids around. I just couldn't take it any longer."

Beverly

When the behavior of Beverly's stepsons began having an adverse effect on her, on her own two sons, and on her marriage, Beverly began to handle the situation much differently. She began to realize that she, too, had rights.

"This is my house, and there are certain things I can't condone. I now tell them: 'There are certain things you can do here and certain things I won't have.' My husband is not reluctant to support me now. The boys sometimes still give me problems. For example, I'll say, 'Hey, pick up your coat and your shoes off the floor and hang them up and put them away,' and the older one acts like I'm holding him up to super-high standards and nobody could live up to them and if you did, you'd be Little Lord Fauntleroy. The other one doesn't want to disappoint anybody, but he acts real hurt afterwards. It's hard to enforce all this, but it's got to be done."

Beverly

Beverly strongly believes that her marriage is better and her stepsons are happier because of the changes that were made, changes which her husband supported. She equates disciplining children with showing love.

"When I was growing up, my father had high standards for all of us, and it took me awhile to understand that that's how he shows his love. I want the boys to be happy, and I think they are. It really is working out."

Beverly, 22, New Jersey

Like Beverly's situation, Dorothy's stepfamily experience is also a "before and after" story but a story that spans two remarriages and two different blended families. Her second marriage, her first stepfamily experience, did not last.

"The stepfamily I was a part of before this one really gave me my views on stepparenting. It was a very painful experience. I was in my twenties and early thirties. My husband then—the biological father of those children—was not willing to take the initiative in the discipline and guidance of his own children. At 27, I was a different person, too, and I couldn't handle it. I have a lot more knowledge now at 42, but we don't get second chances when things don't work out."

Dorothy

Dorothy's third marriage is a happy one, and her relationship with her stepdaughter is good.

"This stepfamily is working. I'm real immediate with my discipline now. I don't sit around and internally hash out what I need to do. I'm immediate with it—and up front. I'm also very honest about why I'm doing something. Much of this came from teaching school and dealing with teenagers. I think if you let kids get away with too much or do everything for them and give them too much, you take them out of the game called life and stunt their growth forever. We've been careful about that with my stepdaughter—and she's made big strides in the last five years. The most important thing about getting into a stepfamily is how much initiative the biological parent is willing to take. My husband does that, and our relationship is an intense one. His daughter is happy, and I truly believe that having an extra parent—a stepmother or a stepfather—can be an enhancement to a child's life."

Dorothy, 42, Oklahoma

We truly can "be an enhancement" in the lives of our stepchildren, and, in helping them to adapt and succeed, we are likely to discover that we are enhancing our own lives as well.

THE SALTZMAN THEORY OF STRUCTURED DISCIPLINE COMMUNICATION

Dr. Earl Saltzman has counseled and worked with hundreds of blended families during the last twenty years. He and his wife Resanne are also experts in child raising from a more personal perspective. Their three children, Beverly, Frank, and David, "grew up" on Structured Discipline Communication, and the individual successes of the Saltzman children are a direct tribute to just how well these strategies and skills work.

The Saltzman Structured Discipline Communication techniques could, in essence, be called "Discipline Communication for Success." The theory has, at its core, the goal of helping children succeed at home so that they will later succeed in life.

Structured Discipline Communication returns to a more traditional method of childrearing. It starts with the premise that parents should set the tone in their families, that parents are in charge, that parents are "the boss." The parents are the teachers, and they must teach the children how to succeed. Most children who learn to succeed in their own home are then able to carry those skills forward into larger areas of life: college, the working world, and, ultimately, marriage and other close personal relationships.

THREE STEPS TO SUCCESS

Men and women who marry for the first time usually have the luxury of adjusting to each other before they have children.

They also have the advantage of adapting to their children at a leisurely pace and discovering, by trial and error, what works and what does not work.

It's much more difficult for remarrying couples. For them, life is like a tape recorder which is turned to "fast forward." Parents and stepparents with children living or visiting in the home must have a plan for dealing with those children and helping them succeed within the family environment.

Structured Discipline Communication provides a positive plan. Putting it into practice involves three steps:

1. We must make sure we have a United Front with our spouse.
2. We must be prepared to tell the children specifically what we expect them to do.
3. We must make certain that the children carry out our requirements.

As stepparents, much of what we personally learned was the direct result of mistakes we initially made. After facing difficult child-related problems and searching for solutions, we found that Structured Discipline Communication made a significant difference in our lives. At its foundation is our strong belief that parents in blended families must form a United Front.

Step 1: *A United Front*

Before we, as parents or stepparents, can successfully establish rules and guidelines which will help our children to succeed, we must first agree with our husbands or wives as to what those rules and guidelines should be. If there is any disagreement between us, the children will immediately spot the area of vulnerability and try to use it against us.

As parents, we need to agree in advance on what specific changes we want to see in a child's behavior, what actions we need to take to accomplish those changes, and how far we are willing to go in order to accomplish them. Then there can be no problem *between us* while the real challenge, the *child's* problem, is being worked.

While establishing and maintaining a United Front is important for all facets of blended family living, it is absolutely essential when dealing with child-related problems. Without it, we have very little chance of changing or improving the problem situation.

Step 2: *Specific Language*

Our children often do not fail to do what we *ask* them to do but instead fail to do what we *want* them to do. Consider these examples:

We told her to come home "early." We didn't tell her a time. She came in at midnight. She said that was "early" for her.

We told him to "get his clothes off the floor." We didn't tell him to hang them up. He threw them on his bed. He said he "got them off the floor."

When we are not specific enough in our communication, our children's behavior frequently disappoints us. Structured Discipline Communication is based on helping our children be successful in doing the things that we ask—*and want*—them to do by being specific in our requests. In order for them to succeed in terms of carrying out a task, we must spell out exactly what we expect from them. We need to learn to be extremely clear and, at the same time, put our messages in positive behavioral terms.

When dealing with children, it is sometimes not enough to simply say "I wish," "I would like," or even "I want"; these comments may not be strong enough or direct enough to elicit the desired actions. The children will want to do what *they* want. They may not choose to do what *we* want them to do, would like them to do, or wish they would do.

When we give instructions to our children, we need to ensure that our messages to them answer the following four questions:

1. *What* task or behavior is to be accomplished?
2. *When* is it to be started?
3. *How well* is it to be done?
4. *When* is it to be completed?

If we are in any way vague about what we expect from our children, they may attempt to twist our words. The more structured and definite our messages are, the less difficulty we will have with them.

The four questions which must be answered whenever we communicate our requirements to a child have one thing in common: specific language. If we want a task started immediately, we need to say: "Be helpful to the family. Be successful. Do this *now*." Otherwise, they will say: "But you didn't say when" or "I was going to do it later." We need to tell them what we expect—and when. It is also important for us to associate the desired behavior with success. Completing the task should have a positive connotation for our children.

We may find it more difficult to feel comfortable in using Structured Discipline Communication with our stepchildren than with our children. Parents and stepparents often have different communication styles with the same children. We relate more easily to our own children than we do to our stepchildren.

Consider the following example:

It's time for seven year old Johnny to go to bed. Johnny does not want to go. Chances are that his father will react quite differently than his stepmother.

Father:	Bedtime. Right now!
Stepmother:	I really think you should go to bed. You'll be tired in the morning.

Johnny's stepmother *suggests* that he go to bed, but she does not *tell* him to go. What she really wants is for Johnny to make *his own* decision to go to bed so that he will like her and not be angry with her for requiring him to go. Unfortunately, her suggestion is not definite enough or direct enough to make Johnny feel that he has to go. He is quite likely to interpret her suggestion as a license to go on doing whatever he's doing.

Johnny's father is more secure in his approach to the problem. He takes it for granted that Johnny loves him and will continue to love him. He also knows that Johnny is not mature enough to make his own decision about when to go to bed. Johnny would choose to stay up late and would then be exhausted and irritable the next day. The decision needs to be made for him.

Chances are, if Johnny's stepmother were dealing with him without her husband's help, she would end up frustrated and angry. Johnny, given a choice, would most likely pursue his own goal, *not going to bed,* rather than hers, *going to bed.* He would probably argue with her in an attempt to get his own way.

Stepmother:	I really think you should go to bed. You'll be tired in the morning.
Johnny:	I don't want to go to bed, and I won't be tired in the morning.

Parents and stepparents are both more effective when they learn to use a structured approach in communicating with their children. Johnny's stepmother should have said: "Johnny, it's time for you to go to bed. Be a success and do so. Now." She has both the right and the responsibility to do this. The word "step" in stepparent does not mean "half parent" or "partial parent." A stepparent is still a parent, and, if Johnny's stepmother learns to be more specific and direct in communicating her requirements, Johnny will begin to accept her as a parent figure. He will also begin to feel more secure because there is now more structure in his life.

When we merely make *requests* of our children, we may be opening the door to manipulation. When we communicate our *requirements* to our children, we are helping to ensure that they are successful in family living.

Step 3: *Following Through*

Step One of Structured Discipline Communication establishes the family environment in which our child can succeed. Step Two gives our children a specific opportunity to succeed. Step Three, following through, is the step that *requires* our children to succeed.

For younger children, Step Three is easy. Dad and Mom mutually decide that their five-year-old daughter will go to bed at eight p.m. They specifically tell her: "It's eight p.m. It's time to go to bed." If she then replies, "I don't want to go to bed," Dad and Mom simply take her by the hand, lead her to the bedroom, and make sure she goes to bed. "You are going to be a success and go to bed now. This is important to Daddy and Mommy, and it will make us all feel good about each other."

When children are adolescents or teenagers, following through can become significantly more difficult. Often the "children" are larger and stronger than we. Even when this is not the case, physical restraints may not be a reasonable approach to the problem. We can't "lead them" into their bedrooms. Adolescents have strong minds of their own. They feel that, emotionally at least, they are as "big" as their parents, that their rights are equal to—or greater than—ours and are not to be usurped. This type of thinking, when expressed or acted upon, can create problems for children and parents alike.

In addition to having to handle the direct problems involving our children's behavior, we also frequently have our spouse's ex-wife or ex-husband waiting in the wings with the inevitable threat: "You can't tell my child what to do!"

Harvey, 45, and his wife, Jocelyn, 35, studied Structured Discipline Communication and were determined to make it work. They had no problems with Steps One or Two but almost gave up on Step Three.

Harvey's two daughters, Tammy, 14, and Wendy, 13, visited one weekend. After dinner on Saturday night, Tammy and Wendy were instructed to clear the table and do the dinner dishes. They refused. They were angry about an earlier argument and were determined not to cooperate in any way with their father and stepmother.

Harvey insisted. "Tammy, Wendy, please do the dishes right now. I care about both of you and want our relationship to be a good one."

Tammy and Wendy still refused to do the dishes and eventually manipulated the situation by phoning their mother to come and pick them up. Their mother, Harvey's ex-wife, complied with their request, and they left their father's house. Harvey was hurt, discouraged—and also infuriated.

Many parents in stepfamilies face this same situation. The children have a potential exit, a loophole, that they do not have in nuclear families: the presence of the "other parent."

If we find ourselves in such a situation, we are then faced with the question: How far am I willing to go to make certain that my requests to the children are met?

Harvey realized that if he did not fully follow through, two serious problems would result:

1. He would not have good feelings about the girls when they visited again. The power would be in their hands. If anything did not meet with their approval, they would simply call their mother to pick them up. As a result, everyone would be walking on eggs.

2. The situation would not be good for the girls either. They would learn that manipulation can work. They would also learn that they do not have to take other people's feelings into consideration. This philosophy would not serve them well later in life.

Harvey decided that, even though it would be difficult, it was important for him to make certain that his daughters followed through on his requests while they were in his home. He knew that this was vital to the future of their relationship. He recognized that his daughters falsely believed that, in life, they shouldn't have to do anything they didn't want to do. Realizing the potential problems in their approach to relationships, Harvey took the following actions:

1. After establishing that his ex-wife would not cooperate with him in handling the girls, he sent her a letter reminding her that his court-ordered visitation was from five p.m. each Friday until five p.m. on Sunday. If she came to his house to pick up the girls on Saturday—or anytime before five on Sunday—she would be in contempt of court.

2. He had a discussion with the girls about the situation. He told them how much he loved them but that he also expected them to honor his requests and he would take any action necessary to ensure that they did so when they were in his home.

Harvey and Jocelyn's situation did improve. As difficult as it was, Harvey took the actions with his girls—and with his ex-wife—that were required to make certain that Tammy and Wendy "succeeded."

We each have to decide who is going to be in control of our homes, the parents or the children. We have to decide how far we are willing to go to make sure that our children succeed—both within our family and in their own future lives.

WHY STRUCTURED DISCIPLINE IS IMPORTANT

One of the reasons that Structured Discipline Communication works is that it gives children a sense of structure in their lives, something children in past generations took for granted. Even adults have difficulty with life's uncertainties and tend to rely on clear and definite structure. If the traffic light is red, we stop. If the light is green, we proceed. But if the light is yellow, we become unsure of what to do. We wonder whether we should stop or try to make it through the intersection before the light turns red. Yellow lights present uncertainties. They confuse us in much the same way that an unstructured life confuses our children.

Mature children can deal with behavioral uncertainties. They can weigh the alternatives and make good choices. Immature children, no matter how intelligent, have difficulty making wise decisions when given a choice between doing what they want to do and what they are being asked to do. In an unstructured situation, they may end up making choices which hurt both themselves and others. As parents, we must help our less mature children learn to make correct choices.

Sometimes this means we have to tell them directly what to do:

"You must finish your homework now, and, after it's finished, we'll watch television together."

"You will mow the lawn before 2:00 p.m., and, when you have finished, I'll be happy to let you use the car."

"Write your thank you notes for your birthday gifts now. When those are finished, we'll celebrate by going out for pizza."

To succeed in life, our children need to learn the most important discipline of all—*self*-discipline. Teaching children to make correct and caring choices early in life helps them to establish a pattern which will carry them into successful adulthood. The choices we initially make for our children will have a direct bearing on the choices they make later in life. We, their parents, are their first teachers, and our homes are their first classrooms.

SEEKING PROFESSIONAL HELP

Most of the effort in building a successful family comes from within the family itself and is a do-it-yourself undertaking, but outside help can make the journey easier.

We asked our survey respondents the question: "Since you married, have you or your spouse ever sought professional counseling regarding your stepfamily situation?"

Fifty percent of the parents and stepparents in our survey replied that they had, on at least one occasion since marriage, sought professional counseling to adjust to stepfamily life.

Ninety-five percent of these parents felt that it had been helpful and, in some cases, had kept the marriage from dissolving.

"We'd all be dead or long separated without counseling."
Betsy, 35, Vermont

"Counseling helps. An outside person notices more because he's not caught up in the situation."
Katy, 40, Florida

"We were trying to keep from splitting up our marriage and started to go to a family counselor. We didn't open up before, and this got our feelings to the surface. I couldn't take it anymore, and I thought the problem was me. The counselor helped us realize it wasn't all me. We should have gone years ago."
Marjorie, 35, Washington

Hundreds of our respondents expressed similar feelings. Professional counseling truly can make a difference when we run into blended family roadblocks.

JOINING A STEPFAMILY SUPPORT GROUP

When we asked our respondents how they felt about support groups, only twenty-six percent replied that they had ever attended one. Many others noted that they were interested but didn't know where to find one.

This can be a problem. When we searched for such a group in Houston several years ago, we couldn't find one either. We did, however, meet a young woman who was interested in starting a stepfamily support group.

On that first evening, seven of us attended, and we all quickly discovered that we had essentially the same problem: children. Our difficulties were really not that unique. We continued to meet every week, and we asked a different family therapist to join us each time. All of the psychologists and counselors who met with us donated their time and guided our discussions, providing feedback. Again and again, someone in the group would say: "I can't believe this! You're going through the same thing I am."

As stepparents, we were all going through the same thing, facing the same stepfamily problems. We all had the same general goal. We all desperately wanted to make our marriages work and create happy, healthy families. As we shared our situation with them and they shared theirs with us, the group became a catalyst for positive change. There was a certain magic in sharing. We laughed together and cried together. Most importantly, we *worked* together to find solutions for our shared problems.

All of us in our group felt that relating to stepchildren was one of the most difficult challenges we had faced in our entire lives—but we learned and we survived. Over time, our children learned as well.

At last, we can look back and happily say: "Look how far we've come!"

10

Keeping Love Alive

How many times have you seriously considered ending your marriage?

This is a difficult question to answer. An honest answer tells us much—not only about our marriages but about ourselves. When we asked our survey respondents this question, 57 percent had seriously considered ending their marriages at least once. Seventeen percent had considered divorce many times and were clearly headed in that direction. On the other hand, 43 percent had never, not even once, considered separation or divorce as an option.

The statistics alone did not surprise us. The fact that *did* startle us was the pattern of differentiation between the couples. The men and women who had considered ending their marriages answered several important questions very differently than the couples who had never considered divorce. We found that the differences were so extreme that we could almost predict which remarriages would flourish and which would dissolve. Clear patterns emerged that showed us what happy, successful couples are doing to make their marriages last and what unhappy, divorce-prone couples are doing to cause their marriages to break up.

In comparing the men and women in these two groups, we found the most extreme differences in five areas:

1. Genuine commitment to the marriage and spouse
2. Sexual satisfaction between the husband and wife
3. Expression of affection in front of others
4. Shared time alone together as a couple
5. Frequent communication of positive messages of caring

All of these areas were joined together by a common thread: the strength of the couple's desire to make marriage work.

When we began *The New American Family,* we called our first chapter "Great Expectations." We wrote about how remarriages start with high hopes and yet fail so routinely. As we begin this last chapter, we are convinced that almost *every* remarriage could be successful if the partners so desired.

In comparing happy remarriages and unhappy remarriages, the differences are much more extreme than we would have imagined. Is there a formula for successful marriage? After analyzing our research data and responses, we believe there really are some answers. At the very least, there are patterns of behavior that will greatly enhance our ability to build a marriage that lasts.

COMMITMENT TO THE MARRIAGE

When we remarried in 1983, we drove a black Ford with a blue and white bumper sticker on the back. The bumper sticker read: "Expect a Miracle!" In reality, we did "expect a miracle." Like so many remarrying couples, we thought blending families together would be simple and easy. Other things in life had *not* been. We had worked to get through college. We had worked to get and hold jobs. We had worked to give our children a good start in school and life. Yet we thought that remarriage and blending our families together would just simply happen. Our own family version of "The Brady Bunch" would be happily replayed day after day. Like so many couples, we did not look at remarriage as something requiring work.

One of our respondents told us:

"I'm sick of hearing that you have to work at marriage. I have to work at my job. I have to work around the house: cooking, cleaning, taking care of the kids. If I have to work at love, too, just forget it!"

Bev, 45, Iowa

Bev's marriage did not last, so she got what she wanted—or did she?

The challenge most stepparents face is grappling with the question: Is it worth it? So many of us wonder: Would I rather be single again? Could I find someone else I could relate to better? Do I really want to work to make this marriage last?

One of our respondents, Ramona, struggled for three years with problems created by her husband's children. Finally, Ramona and her husband, with counseling, worked through their child-related, blended family problems. Yet, just as everything started to go more smoothly in that one important area, Ramona found herself facing more doubts than she had ever had before.

"I look back at our relationship when it began and remember how hopeful and innocent it was. We had no history together yet, no problems, just the hopefulness and the excitement and the passion. All of this hope was run through years of torture and a real horror scene. The kid problems are behind us. From here on out, everything should work out pretty good. The problem is—I look at my husband now and think 'I'm tired. I'm not in it anymore.' The problem did zap a lot of the passion out of our relationship. Zapped the feeling out, zapped the spontaneity out, zapped the camaraderie out. We fought problems for five years and now I'm not even sure I want to play in the game anymore. Who cares? That's where I'm at. We've been fighting tigers for five years, and now that it's stopping, I look at him and go: Do I really want him?"

Ramona, 32, Washington

"Fighting tigers" is very common in blended families, and it does "zap" a lot of the passion out of our relationships. If we are not truly committed to our relationship, our marriage will not last. If we simply "expect a miracle," we ultimately will be disappointed and give up. Living in a blended family is difficult. If we choose to live in a stepfamily, we must understand and accept this.

Once we truly accept the fact that stepfamily living can be difficult, our lives and our remarriages can often become much easier. The reasons this will happen are:

- We will stop asking ourselves: "What's wrong?"
- We will stop telling ourselves: "This *should* be easier. This *should not* be difficult."
- We will start saying: "Making this remarriage a happy one is sometimes really tough, but it's worth it and I will work at it."

As stepparents ourselves, we have done more than our share of moaning and groaning and asking: "Why is it so hard?" We started out "expecting a miracle," but we were not blessed with many miracles. What we finally did get was the realization that having to meet and solve our problems had a special meaning of its own. We strongly feel that working through our challenges was a better decision than going out and starting over again with new partners, new families. If we had chosen that route, the whole blending cycle would have started all over again with new partners, new problems.

Often men and women in second marriages give up much too quickly, telling themselves, "I don't feel like working at it." They tell others that they "fell in love" and then "fell out of love." They say the children caused their problems. In all likelihood, these men and women simply did not take the time to learn what makes a blended family last. If a remarriage seems to call for work and effort, they feel it's easier to just "get out." But, after another divorce, they often regret this decision and wish that they had tried harder.

The first step in keeping love alive in a remarriage comes in telling ourselves: I *will* make this work." There is joy in a lifelong marriage. There is satisfaction in being able to say: "We *made* it work this time."

Erich Fromm, in "The Art of Loving," says:

There is hardly any activity, any enterprise, which is started with such tremendous hopes and expectations, and yet, which fails so regularly, as love. If this were the case with any other activity, people would be eager to know the reasons for the failure, and to learn how one could do better or they would give up the activity. . . . If we want to learn how to love we must proceed in the same way we have to proceed if we want to learn any other art . . . The process of learning an art can be divided into two parts: one, the mastery of the theory; the other, the mastery of the practice . . . . But, aside from learning the theory and practice, there is a third factor necessary to becoming a master in any art—the mastery of the art must be a matter of ultimate concern; there must be nothing else in the world more important than the art.[1]

Can we master the art of loving? We can if it's important to us. Genuine commitment is essential in remarried families.

KEEPING SEX ALIVE

Successful remarried couples keep love alive, and they also keep their sex lives active. According to the participants in our survey, sexual satisfaction in marriage is extremely significant. The statistical correlation between a couple's sexual fulfillment and their stepfamily's blending success is strongly related.

Parents in healthy stepfamilies have frequent and fulfilling sexual relations with their marriage partners. When men and women rate their sex lives with their marital partners as "very good," they also tend to have positive feelings toward their stepchildren. Since they feel loved themselves, it's easier for them to feel loving toward others as well.

In our society, sex is exalted as an expression of love, yet breaking up is the norm for more than half of all remarried couples. Whether or not sex *should be* important is not the question. The fact is: sex is very important to a happy home.

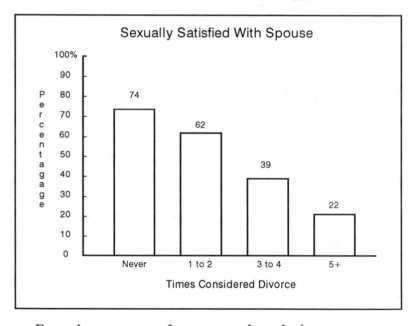

Forty-three percent of our respondents had never, not even once, seriously considered divorce. Looking at a profile of these couples' answers to the questionnaire, one factor that stood out very clearly was that they were sexually active and fulfilled. They felt that marriage—and sex—really can be better the second time around. Seventy-eight percent of them believed that their sexual relationship with their spouse was much better after marriage than before.

These findings were in direct contrast to the responses of the couples who had considered divorce—even those who had only considered it once. Only 39 percent of this group of respondents felt that their sexual relationship with their spouse was better after marriage than before.

The same pattern showed up on the question: "How would you rate your sex life with your spouse?" Seventy-four percent of those who had never considered divorce responded positively. Only 39 percent of those who had considered divorce held positive feelings.

We asked our survey participants the question: "Did you and your partner have a sexual relationship prior to marriage?" Ninety-two percent of them answered "Yes." Seventy-six percent rated their level of premarital sexual activity with their spouse-to-be as "Frequent."

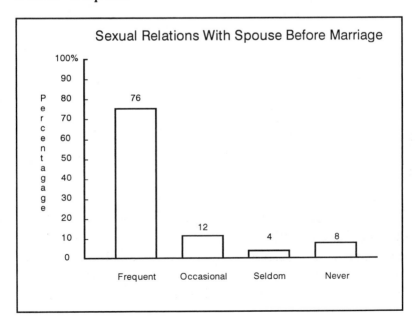

The vast majority of single parents contemplating remarriage *do* participate in sex before marriage. Because of the children, though, premarital sexual relationships are often clandestine, taking on a forbidden aura. Like teenagers who do not want Mom and Dad to know, men and women with children become secretive. Fifty percent of the parents in our survey went to great lengths to keep their premarital sexual activities a secret from their children.

"Because we didn't want the children to know anything about it, we actually rented a motel room."
Sharon, 31, Ohio

"We did it ONLY when the children visited the other parents."
Bob, 37, Indiana

"We did it when they were asleep."
Jack, 32, Texas

"The children never knew."
Gwen, 33, Michigan

"Kept hidden!"
Neil, 47, Florida

After marriage, sexual problems are very different. Physical intimacy no longer has to be "kept hidden," and motels are not necessary. Having an active sex life is easier. However, as the problems involving the presence of the children are solved, new problems arise.

Before marriage, couples do not seem to have to work at creating passionate, romantic escapades nor do they have to worry about keeping that back-seat-of-the-Ford sexual intensity alive. *After* marriage, they do not have to be concerned about the children finding out they are having a sex life.

Yet, for many of our respondents, just as it becomes easier to have an active sex life, desire begins to diminish, and frequency of sexual activity begins to go down. Sex starts to become dull and infrequent. Couples lose their enthusiasm and premarital passion.

We asked our respondents the question: What kinds of things do you do to keep romance alive between you and your spouse? Many responses reflected not only discouragement but a complete giving up.

"I gave up trying in 1978."
Deloris, 54, Indiana

"We do nothing in that area now."
Sheryl, 37, Idaho

"At this point, any romance is completely gone."
Christy, 47, Indiana

A number of these men and women blamed their partner for their unhappy situation.

"He's not romantic or sentimental. I gave up years ago."
Julia, 39, Tennessee

"The bad feelings that have come over the years have interfered with romance for me."

Arlene, 35, Florida

"Romance is almost impossible since he wants to do everything with the children."

Kate, 43, Alabama

It's easy to give up on remarriage. It's easy to give up on romance. It's easy to feel sorry for ourselves and blame our partners for our unhappiness.

It's much harder to take responsibility for our own happiness and to decide that *we* will make the necessary changes in our marriage. It's a lot more difficult to tell ourselves: "I don't like having to put in this much effort, but I'm going to have a physical relationship anyway. The survival of this marriage requires sex, and I'm going to do my best to see that it happens!"

Men and women in successful remarriages put a lot of effort into all areas of their relationship, but sex is inevitably high on their list of priorities.

"We meet at home in the afternoon just to make love."

Helene, 31, California

"We bought a 30 foot sailboat. Sex on the open water is very romantic."

Joanne, 34, Florida

"We do a lot of touching, wear sexy underwear, and watch romantic movies together."

Karen, 30, Florida

"We bathe and shower together. We make sure that we make love on our anniversary every month."

Ruth, 37, Nebraska

"We try to be open to new things like experimenting with different places, positions, and times."

Barbara, 24, South Carolina

"With five kids, things are crazy and we never have time for just us. We had to do something, so we started setting the alarm clock for two a.m. at least once a week."

Shelley, 38, Maine

Many of us will not choose to set our alarm clocks at two a.m., but, if we want our marriage to succeed, we do need to find our own personal answers for keeping the sparks ignited. Sexual satisfaction is important to remarriage success.

SHOWING AFFECTION OPENLY

In addition to keeping our sexual relationship with our spouse alive, we also need to take the time to openly exhibit our feelings of affection. Our husbands and wives feel flattered when they get attention in front of others.

"We talk about our love in front of the kids and everyone else."

Karen, 41, Minnesota

"We kiss and hug each other, morning and night."

Rhoda, 33, California

"We tease each other and make passes secretly in front of others."

Jane, 31, Pennsylvania

"When we're together, even with other people around, we act like we're on a date. I tell him things about his eyes and how much I appreciate him."

Marilyn, 30, Colorado

"When we go out together, like to a party, we make eyes at each other and flirt sexually."

Jerry, 26, Texas

In a world of stepchildren, ex-wives, ex-husbands, and everything else that goes with blending, often we don't feel like kissing and hugging. We don't feel like making eyes at each other. We don't feel like making secret passes at a party. Yet happy remarried couples stress that even if they don't feel like it, they do it anyway.

In strong blended families, couples, in their own personal ways, show affection for each other often—and *in front of others*. Just as a fire needs to be rekindled, love needs to be frequently nurtured. Husbands and wives both need this validation. They need the strength and the value of their relationship to be displayed openly for everyone to see.

In 76 percent of successful marriages, husbands and wives frequently expressed affection toward each other in front of the children. This was in marked contrast to those families which reported ongoing, serious problems. Of that group, only 41 percent demonstrated affection openly.

In our group of respondents who had never seriously considered divorce, 66 percent answered the question with a "1," meaning that they openly expressed affection "*Very* Frequently."

In the group who had considered divorce, only 37 percent answered the question with a "1."

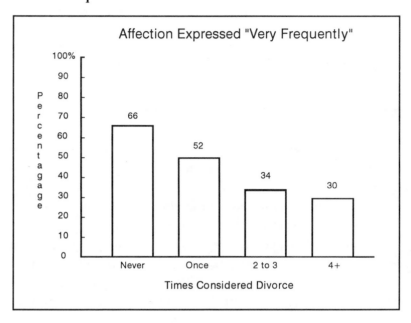

Children also benefit greatly when their parents, their role models, express affection freely at home. Open affection between husband and wife weaves a family identity that gives the children a feeling of stability and security in their daily lives. It is a sign to them that *this family* is sticking together.

Claire Berman, in her book, *Adult Children of Divorce,* talks about the ongoing pain that children of divorce experience. She also discusses the power of a happy remarriage to heal.

"If divorce creates a hole in the heart for many of its children, remarriage can be likened to a life-saving transplant. While the scars do not go away, the wounded youngster . . . may have been given a new lease on a healthier life."[2]

Berman goes on to give examples of children who were introduced to a loving, warm stepfamily atmosphere. Later these children, as adults, felt that watching the affection shown in their blended families gave them positive role models and showed them a better way to make good marriages for themselves. Ultimately, they greatly benefited by stepfamily living.[3]

Couples who openly show affection in front of their children—and others—are happier; they are nurturing their mutual love and are showing their children "a better way."

SPENDING TIME TOGETHER

Couples work at keeping their love alive and their marriage happy in different ways. The common denominator is: they try hard.

Many couples do not make the effort. They don't go out to dinner together or to plays or to sports events. They seldom get away from the kids, and they rarely have fun together. Men and women who face problems in stepfamily life usually find that they spend very little time alone with their spouses. Rather, they become so preoccupied with the problems of the children that no time is left for the marriage itself.

"We don't do anything alone together. We're too tired from work and teenagers."

Julia, 43, Louisiana

"Romance is dead. We just share a house."

Nancy, 43, Georgia

"Romance? What's that? We're too busy trying to solve our problems to have time together as a couple."

Kate, 43, Alabama

Marriages that are this preoccupied with problems are seldom happy marriages. For these couples, life is more of a burden than an adventure. There is no time to loosen up and relax, no time to just play.

Happy couples show a marked contrast. They not only spend time alone together, without the children, but they seek ways to make the shared time fun and sensuous. When they take this private time to nurture each other, they feel nourished themselves.

Lots of little things keep love alive. Couples with happy successful marriages work hard to make their time alone together romantic. We asked our survey participants the question: What kinds of things do you do to keep romance alive? Couples in unsuccessful marriages answered: "We don't."

On the other hand, men and women with happy marriages had lots of suggestions on how to keep the fires burning. These are just a few of them.

Twenty Nine Sparks to Keep the Fires Burning

1. He sends me yellow daffodils in January and red roses in August. (*Sherri*, 29, Ohio)

2. We get a couple movies, make some popcorn, and cuddle in bed. (*Susan*, 35, Washington)

3. We tuck special gifts (like chocolate kisses) under each other's pillows at night. (*Jennifer*, 30, Virginia).

4. We have a party every July and decorate our backyard with colored Christmas lights. (*Mel*, 37, Arizona)

5. Each day we pray together. This keeps us close. (*Charlene*, 46, Tennessee)

6. We light candles almost every night and just talk to each other, drink wine, and listen to country music. (*Bob*, 31, Arkansas)

7. On every holiday, I make him special foods—giant hot dogs on the Fourth of July, hot cross buns on Easter morning, wassail punch on New Year's Day. (*Peggy,* 33, Oregon)

8. We sit in the backyard in our hot tub on cool summer evenings. It's really romantic when there's a full moon. (*Marlene,* 35, Minnesota)

9. We go to a psychologist for counseling and try to understand each other better. (*Annie,* 41, New York)

10. Keeping romance alive is a funny thing. She gets all excited when I help her with the housework—like doing the dishes. When I help her clean the whole house, she's really turned on. (*Dennis,* 60, South Carolina)

11. When the kids are at their dad's, I make a special dinner for him every Saturday night. Lately I've been trying international themes. One Saturday, we had a Japanese dinner on the floor, and I was a geisha girl. Last week I wore a maid's outfit with a frilly white apron and served lots of Danish desserts. (*Melissa,* 27, California)

12. I does sex all kinds of ways. (*Monique,* 34, Texas)

13. We take horseback rides on the beach at sunset. (*Susan,* 35, Washington)

14. We go on fabulous vacations together. Last year we got London theatre tickets. This year we're going to rent a beach house for a week at Martha's Vineyard. (*Barbara,* 46, Pennsylvania)

15. I buy her Elizabeth Taylor's "Passion" perfume. (*Al,* 42, Indiana)

16. I'm a very physical person. I give her great big bear hugs and Swedish massages. Sometimes I wash her hair for her. (*Ben,* 49, Virginia)

17. We loved the film "From Here to Eternity." Whenever we get a chance, we try to find a patch of beach and sand to make love on. (*Candace*, 31, California)

18. We go on wonderful picnics. We spread a lace tablecloth on the grass, get out the silver, the caviar, the champagne—and enjoy. (*Peggy*, 38, Nebraska)

19. I'm pregnant and he loves to put his ear against my stomach and talk to the baby. (*Marcia*, 32, Florida)

20. I dance for him, tease him, wear sexy nightgowns or nothing at all, snuggle close, and ask him to make love to me. (*Lynn*, 38, South Carolina)

21. I pamper her a lot—serve her breakfast in bed and rub her back with Tiger Balm. (*Jerry*, 33, Vermont)

22. I put out good vibes—and it don't take long. (*Willie*, 29, Alabama)

23. We camp in remote areas where swimming nude and sex under the stars is possible. At home we watch wonderful old romantic movies together like "Casablanca" and "For Whom the Bell Tolls". (*Nancy*, 32, Wisconsin)

24. I bake his favorite foods: cherry pie, oatmeal raisin cookies, Swiss chocolate cake. (*Mandy*, 41, Kansas)

25. We try to make our fantasies come true. We search for different places to make love. We also dress up in costumes, undress in sexy ways, tease each other, and talk in special voices, sometimes acting real tough and other times talking baby talk. (*Chakara*, 39, Texas)

26. I give her balloons with paper messages inside telling her how beautiful she is. (*Jack*, 31, Montana)

27. We make a blazing fire on a snowy night. Put a bearskin blanket in front of the fire—and we're ready! (*Patti*, 35, Colorado)

28. I bought a statue of Michelangelo's "David" for our bedroom and said, "This reminds me of you." (*Betty, 38, California*)

29. About once a month, we forget about the laundry and dirty dishes and check into a nice motel. We spend most of our time in bed or out by the pool and order all our meals through room service. (*Sarah*, 37, New Jersey)

Doing special things with our husbands or wives is the cornerstone of remarriage happiness. For our own—and our family's—happiness, we need to take time to play.

COMMUNICATING POSITIVE FEELINGS

In a stepfamily, talking openly and honestly on a daily basis with one's spouse is not an option; it's a necessity. It is also very important to communicate *positive feelings* about our marriage and spouse. There is no way that we can get around talking about problems, chores, and daily living, but we must balance these discussions with positive feedback as well. In the midst of blended family problems, good feelings often get buried and lost.

Couples who get along well together communicate in all sorts of creative ways. They want their marriage partners to feel loved and appreciated, so they make certain to send out strong signals so that their positive, loving messages get transmitted also.

Nearly ten percent of our respondents mentioned that they write personal "love notes" to each other on a frequent basis. Marsha, 30, Colorado, says she leaves lipstick messages saying "I love you" on the bathroom mirror in the mornings. Tami, 38, Ohio, leaves her husband a single flower on his pillow with a romantic note attached. Patricia, 56, Oregon, says: "I send him mushy notes." Donna, 41, Oklahoma, reported that "We still write love letters to each other—even though we live together now."

Rose, 55, Kansas, was one of several women who tucked "I'm thinking of you" notes in her husband's lunch box each day. Judging from the many happy couples who did this, a note saying "I love you" blends very well with a baloney and cheese sandwich!

Our respondents also believe romantic phone calls should be a marital priority.

"He calls me often during the day."
Ann Marie, 30, Ohio

"We leave loving messages on each other's answering machines."
Ridge, 26, California

"She calls me at work just to say 'I love you.'"
Al, 44, Texas

Couples in successful marriages make sure that they talk to each other and express their feelings on a frequent basis. One of our respondents, Jarnette, 35, said: "On Wednesday evenings, we have a standing appointment with a sitter, and we go out and talk, talk, talk."

In blended families, it truly helps to "talk, talk, talk." Many happy couples emphasize how much talking helps them keep their marriages fulfilling.

"We share our thoughts and interests. We find humor in our problems and share a language the children don't know."
Karen, 43, Wisconsin

"We talk and laugh together."

Sharen, 27, Kentucky

"I tell him I love him every day, and I make quiet time for us to be to-gether alone and talk."

Fran, 43, Virginia

"We walk together every night and talk."

Ann, 45, Texas

"She's my best friend. I can tell her anything."

Jack, 32, Texas

A few men and women went even further to *make sure* that communication took place.

"We go away for weekend retreats, and they *force* us to share feelings. After hours of talking, role playing, pretending to be animals, and all the things they have you do, we end up feeling more con-nected to our life together."

Ken, 37, Missouri

"Keeping marriage journals helps us stay tuned in to each other. Sometimes we write down real personal things that are hard to talk about in casual conversation."

Carole, 33, New York

Successful couples talk openly and often, but they also bal-ance their discussions of problems with positive feedback. A lot of communication in blended families revolves around the chil-dren, and that's inevitable. Yet we cannot let these "kid problem" discussions preoccupy us, making our mates feel that they are cared about only on a conditional basis: "I'll love you if you do something about that kid!"

We need to let our husbands and wives know that we care about *them,* that they are special to us, that we are glad they are a part of our lives. Our respondents accomplished this in five ways; these five ways *do* make a difference.

Five Important Factors That Keep Love Alive

1. A genuine commitment to your marriage and spouse.
2. Sexual satisfaction between you and your spouse.
3. Expression of your affection in front of others.
4. Shared time alone together as a couple.
5. Frequent communication of positive messages of caring.

Like Avis, successful remarried couples "try harder."

LIVING HAPPILY EVER AFTER

Personally, we loved writing this last chapter. We feel that it makes a highly positive statement about how hard stepparents in America are trying to make remarriage work. Living in a blended family can be difficult, but, for millions of couples, *The New American Family* is healthy and happy.

After talking to stepparents across the country, our lasting impression is that remarriage can be immensely satisfying in spite of the complications and stresses. Virtually all of our respondents experienced problems as they and their children joined together. Yet many of them worked through these conflicts and created stepfamily harmony. Their personal stories are truly an inspiration. Because they so honestly shared their feelings many of us will travel an easier road as we strive for happy families. We are very grateful for their courage. They made *The New American Family* possible.

As we close our book, we want to thank them and to wish *you* well in your own new American family. May you blend happily and may you always remember the words of *The Rose:*

> *Just remember in the winter*
> *far beneath the bitter snows*
> *Lies the seed that with the sun's love*
> *in the spring becomes the rose.*[4]

Appendices

Appendix A—
The Questionnaire

Our study is the culmination of several years of interest in the intricacies of stepfamily relationships, their problems and their joys. Before we decided to undertake our questionnaire-based survey of American stepfamilies, we had already completed broad general reading on stepfamilies and an intensive library search for material in the academic research area of stepfamily living. We found considerable breadth of treatment but little in the way of valid research on the subject in the general books and magazine articles available on this topic. Conversely, the few statistically valid studies which have been conducted in the area of stepfamily living and reported in academic journals address only extremely narrow topics. (Sociologists study and report on topics such as "The Influence of Stepfamily Living on the Age of First Sexual Experience Among a Cohort of 37 Teen-aged Girls Residing in Harris County, Texas between 1979 and 1984.")

As a result of our reading and library research, we had several goals in mind when we designed our questionnaire and began our search for stepparents and their spouses to help us with our study. First of all, we wanted to *broadly* explore the issues involved in stepfamily life and day-to-day stepfamily living.

Our next objective was to capture the data pertaining to those issues in a quantitative as well as a qualitative format in order that statistical analysis techniques might be applied to the data and conclusions drawn.

Finally, we wanted to ensure that we were including a large *and* diverse sample of stepfamily members in the survey. We wanted respondents from every type of stepfamily and every geographical region of the United States, especially including a random mixture of ages, racial origins, educational levels, occupations, and incomes. We wanted our data, given the one unavoidable caveat of "self-selection," to be statistically valid.

The first result of these objectives was our questionnaire—ten pages in length which is reproduced in the pages of this Appendix.

The second result was our approach to the distribution of those questionnaires. With the exception of a few early test distributions to acquaintances and stepparenting groups (less than 4% of the total survey responses), all of our responses came either through advertisements which we placed in national magazines or through newspaper articles.

The magazines used for this purpose were T*he Saturday Evening Post, Atlantic Monthly, The National Enquirer, Ms.,* and *Psychology Today.* In total, these magazine advertisements accounted for 16% of our total responses.

After six months, however, we were still considerably short of our desired number of 500 questionnaires. At that time, we asked 800 daily newspapers all across the United States to help us by running a short news article on our project. Eighty-five newspapers ran the story, and we received nearly 1,000 inquiries resulting in approximately 500 completed questionnaires from 47 different states.

At that point, 97% of our total responses were from Anglo-Americans. Therefore, our last goal was to get a greater number of responses from minorities. We asked for help from 165 Black newspapers, and 17 responded favorably. Our final totals were 3% Black and 2% from other minority races. Thus, even with our additional efforts, the study primarily reflects the Anglo-American stepparent community. Still, in the areas of age, geographical region, educational level, occupation, and income, our initial objectives were fully met.

Our detailed data has given us the opportunity to view step-families from a number of different vantage points and to draw conclusions which are valid and which successfully cover the spectrum of stepfamily living.

Please complete this questionnaire by filling in the blanks or circling the appropriate response.

OPTIONAL:
Name: _____

If you would like to participate further through a telephone interview, please provide your name and telephone number in the spaces to the right. Confidentiality of all responses is guaranteed.

Phone: _____

Best times
to call: _____

GENERAL INFORMATION

1. Will you be describing a current or former stepfamily?   Current   Former

<u>About you:</u>

2. Sex: _____   3. Your age when you married into stepfamily situation: _____

4. Education (years of school): _____   5. Your own annual income: $_____

6. Your race: White   Black   Hispanic   Oriental   Other

7. # of prior marriages: _____   8. Last marriage ended by: Divorce   Death

9. Occupation: Professional   Management   Technical   Sales   Service

Clerical   Student   Homemaker   Other: _____

<u>About your spouse:</u>

10. Spouse's age when he/she married into stepfamily situation: _____

11. Education (years of school): _____   12. Spouse's annual income: $_____

13. Spouse's race: White   Black   Hispanic   Oriental   Other

14. # of prior marriages: _____   15. Last marriage ended by: Divorce   Death

16. Occupation: Professional   Management   Technical   Sales   Service

Clerical   Student   Homemaker   Other: _____

<u>About your family:</u>

17. Partial Address: City _____ State _____ Zip Code _____

18. Length of Current Marriage (in years): _____

19. After the wedding you lived in: Your former home   Spouse's former home   Other

<u>About the children:</u> (Fill in one section for each child: yours, spouse's, or joint)

		Whose	Lives			Whose	Lives			Whose	Lives
20. Age	Sex	Child	Where	Age	Sex	Child	Where	Age	Sex	Child	Where
a.___	___	___	___	b.___	___	___	___	c.___	___	___	___
d.___	___	___	___	e.___	___	___	___	f.___	___	___	___

<u>About the "other parent"</u>

21. You pay out $_____/year in alimony or you receive $_____/year

22. You pay out $_____/year in child support or you receive $_____/year

23. Your spouse pays $_____/year in alimony or he/she receives $_____/year

24. Your spouse pays $_____/year in child support or he/she receives $_____/year

25. Your ex lives _____ miles away   26. Your spouse's ex lives _____ miles away

ANSWER THE FOLLOWING QUESTIONS BASED ON YOUR FEELINGS PRIOR TO YOUR MARRIAGE

27. Where did you meet your current spouse?

Church   Friends   Relatives   Dating service

School   Work   Club   Bar   Other: _____

28. How realistic were your expectations about marriage the <u>first</u> time you married?

Very realistic 1 2 3 4 5 6 7 8 9 Not realistic

29. How realistic were your expectations for your current marriage?

Very realistic 1 2 3 4 5 6 7 8 9 Not realistic

30. What were your main expectations for your new family?

_____

_____

_____

_____

31. When you decided to marry, did you feel that relating to stepchildren would be difficult or easy?

Very difficult 1 2 3 4 5 6 7 8 9 Very easy

32. Before marriage, how would you have described your ability to handle the stepparent role?

Highly competent 1 2 3 4 5 6 7 8 9 Not competent

33. Was your first meeting with your stepchildren a planned event?

Planned 1 2 3 4 5 6 7 8 9 Not planned

34. How would you describe your first meeting with your stepchildren?

Very positive 1 2 3 4 5 6 7 8 9 Very negative

35. What were the circumstances surrounding that meeting?

_____

_____

_____

36. What part did each of the following play in your decision to remarry?

Strongly considered ... Not considered

a. Need for companionship   1 2 3 4 5 6 7 8 9

b. Need for regular sex partner   1 2 3 4 5 6 7 8 9

c. Another parent for your children   1 2 3 4 5 6 7 8 9

d. A "family" for your children   1 2 3 4 5 6 7 8 9

e. Financial security   1 2 3 4 5 6 7 8 9

f. Love   1 2 3 4 5 6 7 8 9

g. Emotional support/intimacy   1 2 3 4 5 6 7 8 9

h. Increased status   1 2 3 4 5 6 7 8 9

i. Greater community acceptance   1 2 3 4 5 6 7 8 9

j. More advantages for your children   1 2 3 4 5 6 7 8 9

37. How were your children cared for between marriage and remarriage?

By yourself   Other parent   Other relative

Housekeeper   Day care   Other: _____

38. Describe the rules and discipline you imposed on your children before you remarried.

Very Strict   Very casual
1 2 3 4 5 6 7 8 9

39. Did you prepare your children in any special way for the remarriage?

Yes   No

40. If yes, briefly describe how you prepared them.

_____

_____

_____

_____

41. Was living together rather than marrying an option for you?

Was an option   Was not an option
1 2 3 4 5 6 7 8 9

42. Before marriage, was the time you spent with your partner couple oriented or family oriented?

Couple oriented   Family oriented
1 2 3 4 5 6 7 8 9

43. Did you talk with your partner before marriage regarding your feelings about the stepchildren?

Frequently   Never
1 2 3 4 5 6 7 8 9

44. How important was each of the following regarding your step-children?

Very important   Not important

a. That they love me

1 2 3 4 5 6 7 8 9

b. That they respect me

1 2 3 4 5 6 7 8 9

c. That they obey me

1 2 3 4 5 6 7 8 9

d. That they confide in me

1 2 3 4 5 6 7 8 9

e. That they share interests with me

1 2 3 4 5 6 7 8 9

f. That they are honest with me

1 2 3 4 5 6 7 8 9

g. That they are my friends

1 2 3 4 5 6 7 8 9

h. That they like to spend time with me

1 2 3 4 5 6 7 8 9

i. That they are affectionate toward me

1 2 3 4 5 6 7 8 9

j. That they call me "Mom" or "Dad"

1 2 3 4 5 6 7 8 9

k. That they accept my relationship with my spouse (their parent)

1 2 3 4 5 6 7 8 9

l. That they are polite to me

1 2 3 4 5 6 7 8 9

m. That they express gratitude when it is appropriate

1 2 3 4 5 6 7 8 9

n. That they do not criticize me to others

1 2 3 4 5 6 7 8 9

45. How open were you with your spouse about your feelings?

Very open   Not open
1 2 3 4 5 6 7 8 9

46. Did you and your partner have a sexual relationship prior to your marriage?

Frequent relations
1 2 3 4 5 6 7 8 9
No relations

47. If yes, briefly describe how you handled the situation as it affected the children.

_____

_____

_____

_____

PLEASE ANSWER THE REMAINING QUESTIONS BASED ON
YOUR FEELINGS AND EXPERIENCES SINCE MARRIAGE

48. How many hours do you spend alone with your spouse each week?

Less than 1   1-5   5-10   10-15   15-20   Over 20

49. Compared to when you were dating, how would you rate your relationship with your spouse?

Much better
1 2 3 4 5 6 7 8 9
Much worse

50. How would you rate your sex life with your spouse?

Couldn't be better
1 2 3 4 5 6 7 8 9
Couldn't be worse

51. Overall, how satisfied are you in your relationship with your spouse?

Very satisfied
1 2 3 4 5 6 7 8 9
Not at all satisfied

52. How many times have you seriously considered ending your marriage?

Never   Once   2-3 times   4-5 times   More than 5 times

53. What kinds of things do you do to keep romance alive between you and your spouse?

_____

_____

_____

54. Do you ever find yourself competing with your stepchildren for your spouse's attention?

Frequently
1 2 3 4 5 6 7 8 9
Never

55. Is it easy or difficult for you to be open with your spouse regarding his/her children?

Very difficult
1 2 3 4 5 6 7 8 9
Very easy

56. Do you and your spouse express affection toward each other in front of the children?

Frequently
1 2 3 4 5 6 7 8 9
Never

57. Is your sex life with your spouse better or worse while your stepchildren are present in the home?

Much better
1 2 3 4 5 6 7 8 9
Much worse

58. What percentage of your conversation with your spouse centers around the children?

0% 10 20 30 40 50 60 70 80 90 100%

59. Is the money that your spouse spends on his/her children a problem to you?

Frequently
1 2 3 4 5 6 7 8 9
Never

60. Do you and your spouse have separate or joint bank accounts?

Separate   Joint   Both   Neither

61. What percentage of your family's overall basic household expenses do you pay from your own income?

0% 10 20 30 40 50 60 70 80 90 100%

62. Since marriage, has your overall financial situation gotten better or worse?

Much better
1 2 3 4 5 6 7 8

Much worse
9

63. Is your privacy or the privacy of you and your spouse invaded by your own children?

Frequently
1 2 3 4 5 6 7 8

Never
9

64. Is your privacy or the privacy of you and your spouse invaded by your stepchildren?

Frequently
1 2 3 4 5 6 7 8

Never
9

65. How satisfied are you with the relationships you have established with your own children?

Very satisfied
1 2 3 4 5 6 7 8

Not at all satisfied
9

66. How satisfied are you with the relationships you have established with your stepchildren?

Very satisfied
1 2 3 4 5 6 7 8

Not at all satisfied
9

67. How often do you participate in activities with your own children without your spouse?

Daily   2 or 3 times a week   Weekly

2 or 3 times a month   Monthly   Never

68. How often do you participate in activities with your stepchildren without your spouse?

Daily   2 or 3 times a week   Weekly

2 or 3 times a month   Monthly   Never

69. Have your stepchildren treated you better or worse since your marriage than before?

Much better
1 2 3 4 5 6 7 8

Much worse
9

70. After marriage, did you find it easy or difficult to relate to your stepchildren?

Very easy
1 2 3 4 5 6 7 8

Very difficult
9

71. How open are you with your own children about your feelings?

Very open
1 2 3 4 5 6 7 8

Not at all open
9

72. How open are you with your stepchildren about your feelings?

Very open
1 2 3 4 5 6 7 8

Not at all open
9

73. Is it possible to treat your own children and your stepchildren equally?

Very possible
1 2 3 4 5 6 7 8

Not possible
9

74. Do you find it difficult or easy to discipline your own children?

Very easy
1 2 3 4 5 6 7 8

Very difficult
9

75. Do you find it difficult or easy to discipline your stepchildren?

Very easy
1 2 3 4 5 6 7 8

Very difficult
9

76. Do the children complain that their stepparent treats them differently than his/her own children?

Frequently
1 2 3 4 5 6 7 8

Never
9

77. Do you feel your role with your stepchildren is that of a parent or that of a friend?

Mostly a friend
1 2 3 4 5 6 7 8

Mostly a parent
9

78. Do you introduce your stepchildren as your "children"?

Usually 1 2 3 4 5 6 7 8 9 Never

79. If you have a teenage child of the opposite sex as yourself, is he/she jealous of his/her stepparent?

Extremely jealous 1 2 3 4 5 6 7 8 9 Not at all jealous

80. If you have a teenage stepchild of your own sex, do you ever feel jealous of the attention that he/she receives from your spouse?

Frequently 1 2 3 4 5 6 7 8 9 Never

81. Has a sexual attraction between a parent and teenage stepchild ever been a problem in your family?

Yes   No

82. If yes, briefly describe that situation.

_____

_____

_____

_____

83. Are your children and stepchildren more adaptable or less adaptable as a result of stepfamily living?

More adaptable 1 2 3 4 5 6 7 8 9 Less adaptable

84. Are your children and stepchildren more mature or less mature as a result of stepfamily living?

More mature 1 2 3 4 5 6 7 8 9 Less mature

85. Do you get adequate recognition from your own children for the things you do for them?

Always 1 2 3 4 5 6 7 8 9 Never

86. Do you get adequate recognition from your stepchildren for the things you do for them?

Always 1 2 3 4 5 6 7 8 9 Never

87. Have any of the children shown any hostility toward their stepsisters or stepbrothers?

Frequently 1 2 3 4 5 6 7 8 9 Never

88. Is competition between children a problem in your stepfamily?

Frequently 1 2 3 4 5 6 7 8 9 Never

89. Do the children treat their "natural" brothers/sisters better or worse than their stepbrothers and stepsisters?

Much better 1 2 3 4 5 6 7 8 9 Much worse

90. How would you describe the relationship between your children and their stepbrothers/stepsisters?

Couldn't be better 1 2 3 4 5 6 7 8 9 Couldn't be worse

91. What have you found to be the major problems between your children and their stepbrothers/stepsisters?

_____

_____

92. Has a romantic or sexual attraction between stepbrothers and stepsisters ever been a problem?

_____

_____

_____

93. Do you feel that the sex of a stepchild makes a difference in relating
successfully? If so, describe your
reasons. _____

_____

_____

_____

94. Do you feel that the age of a stepchild makes a difference in relating
successfully? If so, describe your
reasons. _____

_____

_____

_____

95. How do you deal with anger and
aggression between your children
and stepchildren? _____

_____

_____

_____

96. Describe briefly how your stepfamily
handles holidays. _____

_____

_____

_____

97. Have there been changes in child
custody or residency during your
marriage? If so, briefly describe
those changes. _____

_____

_____

_____

_____

	Daily	Weekly	Monthly	1 or 2 times a year

98. How often do you have contact with
your ex-spouse?

Less than once a year   Never

99. Do you consider your ex-spouse
to be your friend?

Close
friend   Not a friend
1 2 3 4 5 6 7 8 9

100. Does your current spouse like your
ex-spouse?

Very
much   Not at all
1 2 3 4 5 6 7 8 9

101. Does your spouse's ex-spouse like
you?

Very
much   Not at all
1 2 3 4 5 6 7 8 9

102. If you pay alimony or child support, are these payments a financial hardship to you?

Very much so 1 2 3 4 5 6 7 8 9 Not at all

103. If you pay alimony or child support, have these payments caused problems between you and your current spouse?

Frequently 1 2 3 4 5 6 7 8 9 Never

104. If you receive alimony/child support, have these payments caused problems between you and your current spouse?

Frequently 1 2 3 4 5 6 7 8 9 Never

105. What percentage of the dealings with your spouse's ex-spouse do you personally handle?

0% 10 20 30 40 50 60 70 80 90 100%

106. What percentage of the dealings with your own ex-spouse do you personally handle?

0% 10 20 30 40 50 60 70 80 90 100%

107. Do your children transmit messages between you and your ex-spouse?

Frequently 1 2 3 4 5 6 7 8 9 Never

108. Do your stepchildren transmit messages between your spouse and his/her ex-spouse?

Frequently 1 2 3 4 5 6 7 8 9 Never

109. Is your ex-spouse helpful in working with you for the benefit of your children?

Very helpful 1 2 3 4 5 6 7 8 9 Not helpful

110. Is your spouse's ex-spouse helpful in working with your spouse for the benefit of your stepchildren?

Very helpful 1 2 3 4 5 6 7 8 9 Not helpful

111. Do your stepchildren verbally compare you in an unfavorable way to their "natural" mother/father?

Frequently 1 2 3 4 5 6 7 8 9 Never

112. Do you ever feel that you have to compete with your spouse's ex-spouse?

Frequently 1 2 3 4 5 6 7 8 9 Never

113. Do your own children ever fantasize about their "real" parents getting back together again?

Frequently 1 2 3 4 5 6 7 8 9 Never

114. Do your stepchildren ever fantasize about their "real" parents getting back together again?

Frequently 1 2 3 4 5 6 7 8 9 Never

115. How would you describe your relationship with your ex-spouse? _____

_____

_____

116. How would you describe your relationship with your spouse's ex-spouse? _____

_____

_____

_____

117. If your minor children live with you, how often does your ex-spouse see your children?

Daily Weekly Monthly 1 or 2 times a year

Less than once a year Never

118. If your minor children do not live with you, how often do you see them?

Daily   Weekly   Monthly   1 or 2 times a year

Less than once a year   Never

119. If your minor stepchildren live with you, how often does your spouse's ex-spouse see them?

Daily   Weekly   Monthly   1 or 2 times a year

Less than once a year   Never

120. If your minor stepchildren do not live with you, how often does your spouse see them?

Daily   Weekly   Monthly   1 or 2 times a year

Less than once a year   Never

121. Do your stepchildren portray you accurately to their "other" parent?

Very accurately								Not accurately
1	2	3	4	5	6	7	8	9

122. How well have your parents and your spouse's parents accepted your marriage and stepchildren?

_____

_____

_____

_____

123. If your parents are living, how often do your minor children see or visit them?

Daily   Weekly   Monthly   1 or 2 times a year

Less than once a year   Never

124. If your parents are living, how often do your minor stepchildren see or visit them?

Daily   Weekly   Monthly   1 or 2 times a year

Less than once a year   Never

125. If your parents are living, do they treat their "natural" grand-children and step-grandchildren equally (with gifts and so forth)?

Always								Never
1	2	3	4	5	6	7	8	9

126. If your spouse's parents are living, how often do your minor stepchildren see or visit them?

Daily   Weekly   Monthly   1 or 2 times a year

Less than once a year   Never

127. If your spouse's parents are living, how often do your own minor children see or visit them?

Daily   Weekly   Monthly   1 or 2 times a year

Less than once a year   Never

128. If your spouse's parents are living, do they treat their "natural" grandchildren and step-grandchildren equally?

Always								Never
1	2	3	4	5	6	7	8	9

129. If your ex-spouse's parents are living, how often do your minor children see or visit them?

Daily   Weekly   Monthly   1 or 2 times a year

Less than once a year   Never

130. Since you married, have you or your spouse ever sought professional counseling regarding your stepfamily situation?

Frequently   A few times   Once   Never

131. Since you married, have you or your spouse ever attended workshops, classes, or discussion groups on stepfamily living?

Frequently   A few times   Once   Never

132. Since you married, have any of your children or stepchildren required professional counseling in order to adjust to stepfamily living?

Frequently   A few times   Once   Never

133. What is your opinion of counseling, discussion groups, etc. as an aid in working out stepfamily problems? _____

_____

_____

134. Do visiting children/stepchildren receive more attention or less attention than the children/step-children who live in your home?

Much more — 1 2 3 4 5 6 7 8 9 — Much less

135. Do visiting children/stepchildren participate more often or less often in household chores than children/stepchildren who live in your home?

Much more — 1 2 3 4 5 6 7 8 9 — Much less

136. Do visiting children/stepchildren have more rules or fewer rules than children/stepchildren who live in your home?

More rules — 1 2 3 4 5 6 7 8 9 — Fewer rules

137. Are visiting children/stepchildren punished more often or less often than children/stepchildren who live in your home?

More often — 1 2 3 4 5 6 7 8 9 — Less often

138. Do you and your spouse differ on how to handle problems concerning the children/stepchildren who live with you?

Frequently — 1 2 3 4 5 6 7 8 9 — Never

139. Do you and your spouse differ on how to handle problems concerning visiting children/stepchildren?

Frequently — 1 2 3 4 5 6 7 8 9 — Never

140. Do you see any major differences in relating to visiting children/stepchildren and in relating to children/stepchildren who live in your home? _____

_____

_____

SUMMARY

List the positive feelings you have about your stepfamily experiences:

_____

_____

_____

_____

_____

List the negative feelings you have about your stepfamily experiences:

_____

_____

_____

_____

_____

Appendix B —
Selected Statistics

Note: Percentage data is based on the number of respondents who answered the specific question—not on the total number of respondents.

FOLLOWING ANSWERS BASED ON FEELINGS PRIOR TO MARRIAGE:

28. How realistic were your expectations about marriage the <u>first</u> time you married?

Very realistic   Not realistic

	1	2	3	4	5	6	7	8	9
%	16	7	10	7	12	7	14	10	17 %

29. How realistic were your expectations for your current marriage?

Very realistic   Not realistic

	1	2	3	4	5	6	7	8	9
%	26	21	18	7	12	5	5	2	4

31. When you decided to marry, did you feel that relating to stepchildren would be difficult or easy?

Very difficult   Very easy

	1	2	3	4	5	6	7	8	9
%	6	3	11	10	23	8	18	10	11 %

32. Before marriage, how would you have described your ability to handle the stepparent role?

Highly competent   Not competent

	1	2	3	4	5	6	7	8	9
%	18	20	24	9	13	4	5	3	4 %

33. Was your first meeting with your stepchildren a planned event?

Planned   Not planned

	1	2	3	4	5	6	7	8	9
%	46	8	7	2	4	1	4	4	24 %

34. How would you describe your first meeting with your stepchildren?

Very positive   Very negative

	1	2	3	4	5	6	7	8	9
%	28	18	17	8	16	4	3	1	5 %

36. What part did each of the following play in your decision to remarry?

Strongly considered   Not considered

a. Need for companionship

	1	2	3	4	5	6	7	8	9
%	40	18	17	6	8	1	4	2	4 %

b. Need for regular sex partner

	1	2	3	4	5	6	7	8	9
%	14	12	13	10	20	5	8	6	12 %

c. Another parent for your children

	1	2	3	4	5	6	7	8	9
%	12	10	9	6	12	2	8	7	34 %

d. A "family" for your children

	1	2	3	4	5	6	7	8	9
%	20	8	9	6	11	3	7	6	30 %

e. Financial security

	1	2	3	4	5	6	7	8	9
%	14	6	9	11	15	3	9	8	25 %

f. Love

	1	2	3	4	5	6	7	8	9
%	67	17	5	3	4	1	1	1	1 %

g. Emotional support/intimacy

	1	2	3	4	5	6	7	8	9
%	57	19	11	4	4	1	1	2	1 %

h. Increased status

	1	2	3	4	5	6	7	8	9
%	4	3	5	4	14	4	7	9	50 %

i. Greater community acceptance

	1	2	3	4	5	6	7	8	9
%	5	2	3	6	10	3	5	10	56 %

j. More advantages for your children

	1	2	3	4	5	6	7	8	9
%	11	7	9	7	15	3	5	7	36 %

38. Describe the rules and discipline you imposed on your children before you remarried.

Very Strict								Very casual
1	2	3	4	5	6	7	8	9
% 3	8	18	19	26	6	12	4	4 %

39. Did you prepare your children in any special way for the remarriage?

Yes 60%	No 40%

41. Was living together rather than marrying an option for you?

Was an option								Was not an option
1	2	3	4	5	6	7	8	9
% 35	5	4	2	5	1	3	3	42 %

42. Before marriage, was the time you spent with your partner couple oriented or family oriented?

Couple oriented								Family oriented
1	2	3	4	5	6	7	8	9
% 19	8	10	8	24	5	7	7	12 %

43. Did you talk with your partner before marriage regarding your feelings about the stepchildren?

Frequently								Never
1	2	3	4	5	6	7	8	9
% 26	13	16	11	11	4	8	5	6 %

44. How important was each of the following regarding your stepchildren?

a. That they love me

Very important								Not important
1	2	3	4	5	6	7	8	9
% 18	8	10	13	18	4	10	7	12 %

b. That they respect me

1	2	3	4	5	6	7	8	9
% 52	20	12	5	5	1	2	1	2 %

c. That they obey me

1	2	3	4	5	6	7	8	9
% 31	18	16	9	12	4	2	2	6 %

d. That they confide in me

1	2	3	4	5	6	7	8	9
% 10	5	13	13	22	8	10	6	13 %

e. That they share interests with me

1	2	3	4	5	6	7	8	9
% 9	6	18	14	22	8	6	4	13 %

f. That they are honest with me

1	2	3	4	5	6	7	8	9
% 67	16	9	2	2	1	1	0	2 %

g. That they are my friends

1	2	3	4	5	6	7	8	9
% 26	12	15	10	19	3	5	4	6 %

h. That they like to spend time with me

1	2	3	4	5	6	7	8	9
% 18	11	17	12	21	5	5	4	7 %

i. That they are affectionate toward me

1	2	3	4	5	6	7	8	9
% 10	9	13	12	23	6	9	8	10 %

j. That they call me "Mom" or "Dad"

1	2	3	4	5	6	7	8	9
% 3	3	2	2	8	1	5	5	71 %

k. That they accept my relationship with my spouse (their parent)

1	2	3	4	5	6	7	8	9
% 70	14	7	3	3	1	1	0	1 %

l. That they are polite to me

1	2	3	4	5	6	7	8	9
% 51	19	14	5	7	1	2	0	1 %

m. That they express gratitude when it is appropriate

1	2	3	4	5	6	7	8	9
% 24	17	18	11	18	3	4	2	3 %

n. That they do not criticize me to others

1	2	3	4	5	6	7	8	9
% 27	12	13	7	17	4	8	2	10 %

45. How open were you with your spouse about your feelings?

Very open
| 1 | 2 | 3 | 4 | 5 | 6 | 7 | 8 | 9 Not open |
| % 49 | 18 | 14 | 6 | 5 | 2 | 4 | 1 | 1 % |

46. Did you and your partner have a sexual relationship prior to your marriage?

Frequent relations
| 1 | 2 | 3 | 4 | 5 | 6 | 7 | 8 | 9 No relations |
| % 54 | 11 | 11 | 4 | 5 | 2 | 2 | 3 | 8 % |

FOLLOWING ANSWERS BASED ON FEELINGS/EXPERIENCES SINCE MARRIAGE:

48. How many hours do you spend alone with your spouse each week?

Less than 1	1-5	5-10	10-15	15-20	Over 20
3%	28%	22%	13%	12%	22%

49. Compared to when you were dating, how would you rate your relationship with your spouse?

Much better
| 1 | 2 | 3 | 4 | 5 | 6 | 7 | 8 | 9 Much worse |
| % 24 | 15 | 16 | 8 | 12 | 8 | 6 | 3 | 8 % |

50. How would you rate your sex life with your spouse?

Couldn't be better
| 1 | 2 | 3 | 4 | 5 | 6 | 7 | 8 | 9 Couldn't be worse |
| % 22 | 14 | 17 | 8 | 16 | 6 | 8 | 4 | 5 % |

51. Overall, how satisfied are you in your relationship with your spouse?

Very satisfied
| 1 | 2 | 3 | 4 | 5 | 6 | 7 | 8 | 9 Not at all satisfied |
| % 36 | 19 | 14 | 5 | 6 | 6 | 6 | 2 | 6 % |

52. How many times have you seriously considered ending your marriage?

Never	Once	2-3 times	4-5 times	More than 5 times
43%	13%	21%	6%	17%

54. Do you ever find yourself competing with your stepchildren for your spouse's attention?

Frequently
| 1 | 2 | 3 | 4 | 5 | 6 | 7 | 8 | 9 Never |
| % 9 | 6 | 11 | 10 | 9 | 4 | 12 | 12 | 27 % |

55. Is it easy or difficult for you to be open with your spouse regarding his/her children?

Very difficult
| 1 | 2 | 3 | 4 | 5 | 6 | 7 | 8 | 9 Very easy |
| % 8 | 6 | 11 | 6 | 8 | 5 | 13 | 15 | 28 % |

56. Do you and your spouse express affection toward each other in front of the children?

Frequently
| 1 | 2 | 3 | 4 | 5 | 6 | 7 | 8 | 9 Never |
| % 49 | 17 | 15 | 6 | 7 | 2 | 1 | 2 | 1 % |

57. Is your sex life with your spouse better or worse while your stepchildren are present in the home?

Much better
| 1 | 2 | 3 | 4 | 5 | 6 | 7 | 8 | 9 Much worse |
| % 2 | 1 | 2 | 5 | 52 | 10 | 9 | 8 | 11 % |

58. What percentage of your conversation with your spouse centers around the children?

0%	10	20	30	40	50	60	70	80	90	100%
% 0	7	9	17	16	19	11	10	8	2	1 %

59. Is the money that your spouse spends on his/her children a problem to you?

Frequently
| 1 | 2 | 3 | 4 | 5 | 6 | 7 | 8 | 9 Never |
| % 5 | 4 | 8 | 8 | 9 | 4 | 11 | 12 | 39 % |

62. Since marriage, has your overall financial situation gotten better or worse?

Much better
| 1 | 2 | 3 | 4 | 5 | 6 | 7 | 8 | 9 Much worse |
| % 32 | 9 | 14 | 9 | 16 | 5 | 6 | 3 | 6 % |

63. Is your privacy or the privacy of you and your spouse invaded by your own children?

Frequently   Never

1	2	3	4	5	6	7	8	9
% 7	8	12	11	15	3	14	9	21 %

64. Is your privacy or the privacy of you and your spouse invaded by your stepchildren?

Frequently   Never

1	2	3	4	5	6	7	8	9
% 7	7	14	12	15	5	13	10	17 %

65. How satisfied are you with the relationships you have established with your own children?

Very satisfied   Not at all satisfied

1	2	3	4	5	6	7	8	9
% 42	23	15	5	4	3	4	3	1 %

66. How satisfied are you with the relationships you have established with your stepchildren?

Very satisfied   Not at all satisfied

1	2	3	4	5	6	7	8	9
% 16	11	15	10	10	6	12	6	14 %

67. How often do you participate in activities with your own children without your spouse?

Daily	2 or 3 times a week	Weekly
25%	19%	12%
2 or 3 times a month	Monthly	Never
14%	16%	14%

68. How often do you participate in activities with your stepchildren without your spouse?

Daily	2 or 3 times a week	Weekly
12%	10%	12%
2 or 3 times a month	Monthly	Never
12%	25%	29%

69. Have your stepchildren treated you better or worse since your marriage than before?

Much better   Much worse

1	2	3	4	5	6	7	8	9
% 9	9	16	9	28	4	10	3	12 %

70. After marriage, did you find it easy or difficult to relate to your stepchildren?

Very easy   Very difficult

1	2	3	4	5	6	7	8	9
% 13	11	14	6	13	11	11	6	15 %

71. How open are you with your own children about your feelings?

Very open   Not at all open

1	2	3	4	5	6	7	8	9
% 41	23	15	6	6	3	2	2	2 %

72. How open are you with your stepchildren about your feelings?

Very open   Not at all open

1	2	3	4	5	6	7	8	9
% 19	12	15	11	9	9	6	8	11 %

73. Is it possible to treat your own children and your stepchildren equally?

Very possible   Not possible

1	2	3	4	5	6	7	8	9
% 23	12	12	6	8	6	8	6	19 %

74. Do you find it difficult or easy to discipline your own children?

Very easy   Very difficult

1	2	3	4	5	6	7	8	9
% 32	20	16	6	9	6	7	2	2 %

75. Do you find it difficult or easy to discipline your stepchildren?

Very easy   Very difficult

1	2	3	4	5	6	7	8	9
% 11	7	11	10	11	10	10	8	22 %

76. Do the children complain that their stepparent treats them differently than his/her own children?

Frequently   Never

1	2	3	4	5	6	7	8	9
% 11	4	5	7	8	4	7	16	38 %

77. Do you feel your role with your stepchildren is that of a parent or that of a friend?

	Mostly a friend								Mostly a parent
	1	2	3	4	5	6	7	8	9
%	15	9	7	5	18	5	10	15	16 %

78. Do you introduce your stepchildren as your "children"?

	Usually								Never
	1	2	3	4	5	6	7	8	9
%	37	11	8	4	8	2	3	3	24 %

79. If you have a teenage child of the opposite sex as yourself, is he/she jealous of his/her stepparent?

	Extremely jealous								Not at all jealous
	1	2	3	4	5	6	7	8	9
%	8	4	8	5	15	3	8	9	40 %

80. If you have a teenage stepchild of your own sex, do you ever feel jealous of the attention that he/she receives from your spouse?

	Frequently								Never
	1	2	3	4	5	6	7	8	9
%	4	4	8	8	8	4	9	11	44 %

83. Are your children and stepchildren more adaptable or less adaptable as a result of stepfamily living?

	More adaptable								Less adaptable
	1	2	3	4	5	6	7	8	9
%	22	18	21	12	16	3	3	2	3 %

84. Are your children and stepchildren more mature or less mature as a result of stepfamily living?

	More mature								Less mature
	1	2	3	4	5	6	7	8	9
%	20	16	20	12	20	3	3	2	4 %

85. Do you get adequate recognition from your own children for the things you do for them?

	Always								Never
	1	2	3	4	5	6	7	8	9
%	20	16	23	10	11	6	8	3	3 %

86. Do you get adequate recognition from your stepchildren for the things you do for them?

	Always								Never
	1	2	3	4	5	6	7	8	9
%	8	9	17	11	12	8	9	13	13 %

87. Have any of the children shown any hostility toward their stepsisters or stepbrothers?

	Frequently								Never
	1	2	3	4	5	6	7	8	9
%	9	7	10	11	13	5	7	12	26 %

88. Is competition between children a problem in your stepfamily?

	Frequently								Never
	1	2	3	4	5	6	7	8	9
%	11	7	11	7	11	4	9	14	26 %

89. Do the children treat their "natural" brothers/sisters better or worse than their stepbrothers and stepsisters?

	Much better								Much worse
	1	2	3	4	5	6	7	8	9
%	11	8	8	7	54	4	3	1	4 %

90. How would you describe the relationship between your children and their stepbrothers/stepsisters?

	Couldn't be better								Couldn't be worse
	1	2	3	4	5	6	7	8	9
%	15	16	19	6	26	6	7	2	3 %

98. How often do you have contact with your ex-spouse?

Daily	Weekly	Monthly	1 or 2 times a year
1%	14%	20%	22%

Less than once a year	Never
12%	31%

99. Do you consider your ex-spouse to be your friend?

	Close friend								Not a friend
	1	2	3	4	5	6	7	8	9
%	4	2	7	6	10	4	9	9	49 %

100. Does your current spouse like your ex-spouse?

	Very much								Not at all
	1	2	3	4	5	6	7	8	9
%	4	2	5	4	21	5	11	10	38 %

101. Does your spouse's ex-spouse like you?

	Very much								Not at all	
	1	2	3	4	5	6	7	8	9	
%	3	3	7	7	18	6	9	11	36	%

102. If you pay alimony or child support, are these payments a financial hardship to you?

	Very much so								Not at all	
	1	2	3	4	5	6	7	8	9	
%	15	10	15	9	15	3	6	10	17	%

103. If you pay alimony or child support, have these payments caused problems between you and your current spouse?

	Frequently								Never	
	1	2	3	4	5	6	7	8	9	
%	12	2	8	9	7	3	6	15	38	%

104. If you receive alimony/child support, have these payments caused problems between you and your current spouse?

	Frequently								Never	
	1	2	3	4	5	6	7	8	9	
%	7	1	6	4	7	2	7	12	54	%

105. What percentage of the dealings with your spouse's ex-spouse do you personally handle?

	0%	10	20	30	40	50	60	70	80	90	100%
%	42	19	8	5	2	6	3	4	3	5	3 %

106. What percentage of the dealings with your own ex-spouse do you personally handle?

	0%	10	20	30	40	50	60	70	80	90	100%
%	11	3	2	3	1	2	2	2	7	17	50 %

107. Do your children transmit messages between you and your ex-spouse?

	Frequently								Never	
	1	2	3	4	5	6	7	8	9	
%	6	3	5	5	10	6	7	20	38	%

108. Do your stepchildren transmit messages between your spouse and his/her ex-spouse?

	Frequently								Never	
	1	2	3	4	5	6	7	8	9	
%	16	6	7	7	11	4	8	14	27	%

109. Is your ex-spouse helpful in working with you for the benefit of your children?

	Very helpful								Not helpful	
	1	2	3	4	5	6	7	8	9	
%	14	8	7	7	7	3	8	9	37	%

110. Is your spouse's ex-spouse helpful in working with your spouse for the benefit of your stepchildren?

	Very helpful								Not helpful	
	1	2	3	4	5	6	7	8	9	
%	8	4	7	6	6	4	11	11	43	%

111. Do your stepchildren verbally compare you in an unfavorable way to their "natural" mother/father?

	Frequently								Never	
	1	2	3	4	5	6	7	8	9	
%	6	2	6	4	8	2	9	15	48	%

112. Do you ever feel that you have to compete with your spouse's ex-spouse?

	Frequently								Never	
	1	2	3	4	5	6	7	8	9	
%	7	3	7	5	4	2	7	16	49	%

113. Do your own children ever fantasize about their "real" parents getting back together again?

	Frequently								Never	
	1	2	3	4	5	6	7	8	9	
%	7	6	4	6	9	3	6	14	45	%

114. Do your stepchildren ever fantasize about their "real" parents getting back together again?

	Frequently								Never	
	1	2	3	4	5	6	7	8	9	
%	12	7	6	8	13	2	7	13	32	%

117. If your minor children live with you, how often does your ex-spouse see your children?

Daily	Weekly	Monthly	1 or 2 times a year
4%	16%	21%	29%

	Less than once a year	Never
	7%	23%

118. If your minor children do not live with you, how often do you see them?

Daily	Weekly	Monthly	1 or 2 times a year
7%	32%	32%	18%
	Less than once a year		Never
	8%		3%

119. If your minor stepchildren live with you, how often does your spouse's ex-spouse see them?

Daily	Weekly	Monthly	1 or 2 times a year
3%	23%	30%	26%
	Less than once a year		Never
	7%		11%

120. If your minor stepchildren do not live with you, how often does your spouse see them?

Daily	Weekly	Monthly	1 or 2 times a year
3%	35%	31%	23%
	Less than once a year		Never
	4%		4%

121. Do your stepchildren portray you accurately to their "other" parent?

Very accurately								Not accurately
1	2	3	4	5	6	7	8	9
% 10	9	13	8	26	7	9	6	12 %

123. If your parents are living, how often do your minor children see or visit them?

Daily	Weekly	Monthly	1 or 2 times a year
6%	19%	27%	34%
	Less than once a year		Never
	12%		2%

124. If your parents are living, how often do your minor stepchildren see or visit them?

Daily	Weekly	Monthly	1 or 2 times a year
1%	9%	21%	42%
	Less than once a year		Never
	15%		12%

125. If your parents are living, do they treat their "natural" grandchildren and step-grandchildren equally (with gifts and so forth)?

Always								Never
1	2	3	4	5	6	7	8	9
% 39	11	8	5	5	6	7	6	13 %

126. If your spouse's parents are living, how often do your minor stepchildren see or visit them?

Daily	Weekly	Monthly	1 or 2 times a year
4%	13%	25%	38%
	Less than once a year		Never
	16%		4%

127. If your spouse's parents are living, how often do your own minor children see or visit them?

Daily	Weekly	Monthly	1 or 2 times a year
2%	13%	23%	34%
	Less than once a year		Never
	17%		11%

128. If your spouse's parents are living, do they treat their "natural" grandchildren and step-grandchildren equally?

Always								Never
1	2	3	4	5	6	7	8	9
% 33	12	10	5	6	5	12	3	14 %

129. If your ex-spouse's parents are living, how often do your minor children see or visit them?

Daily	Weekly	Monthly	1 or 2 times a year
2%	9%	20%	34%
	Less than once a year		Never
	22%		13%

130. Since you married, have you or your spouse ever sought professional counseling regarding your stepfamily situation?

Frequently	A few times	Once	Never
12%	24%	14%	50%

131. Since you married, have you or your spouse ever attended workshops, classes, or discussion groups on stepfamily living?

Frequently	A few times	Once	Never
4%	13%	9%	74%

132. Since you married, have any of your children or stepchildren required professional counseling in order to adjust to stepfamily living?

Frequently	A few times	Once	Never
9%	17%	12%	62%

134. Do visiting children/stepchildren receive more attention or less attention than the children/stepchildren who live in your home?

Much more								Much less
1	2	3	4	5	6	7	8	9
% 9	7	13	10	52	4	3	2	0 %

135. Do visiting children/stepchildren participate more often or less often in household chores than children/stepchildren who live in your home?

Much more								Much less
1	2	3	4	5	6	7	8	9
% 4	2	2	3	43	7	11	9	19 %

136. Do visiting children/stepchildren have more rules or fewer rules than children/stepchildren who live in your home?

More rules								Fewer rules
1	2	3	4	5	6	7	8	9
% 3	1	1	1	56	6	8	10	14 %

137. Are visiting children/stepchildren punished more often or less often than children/stepchildren who live in your home?

More often								Less often
1	2	3	4	5	6	7	8	9
% 1	1	3	2	49	4	11	8	21 %

138. Do you and your spouse differ on how to handle problems concerning the children/stepchildren who live with you?

Frequently								Never
1	2	3	4	5	6	7	8	9
% 16	10	16	13	11	5	10	13	6 %

139. Do you and your spouse differ on how to handle problems concerning visiting children/stepchildren?

Frequently								Never
1	2	3	4	5	6	7	8	9
% 17	7	12	13	14	3	10	13	11 %

Appendix C —
Chapter Notes

Our Story

1. Elizabeth Einstein (interview), "Stepfamilies—Dealing with Anger and Disappointment", *U.S. News and World Report*, Vol. 92, No. 2 (17, January 1983), pp. 67-68.

2. Cherlin, Andrew and James McCarthy, "Remarried Couple Households: Data from the June 1980 Current Population Survey," *Journal of Marriage and the Family*, Vol. 47 (February 1985), pp. 23-30.

3. Norton, Arthur J. and Jeanne E. Moorman, "Current Trends in Marriage and Divorce among American Women," *Journal of Marriage and the Family*, Vol. 49 (February 1987), pp. 3-14.

4. White, Lynn K. and Alan Booth, "The Quality and Stability of Remarriages: The Role of Stepchildren," *American Sociological Review*, Vol. 50 (October 1985), pp. 689-698.

Chapter 1

1. Norton, Arthur J. and Jeanne E. Moorman, February 1987.

2. Sands, Melissa, *The Second Wife's Survival Manual*, New York: Berkley Books, 1982, p. 182. See also White, Lynn K. and Alan Booth, October 1985.

3. Norton, Arthur J. and Jeanne E. Moorman, February 1987.

4. Liebowitz, Michael R., M.D., *The Chemistry of Love,* Boston: Little, Brown and Company, 1983.

Chapter 2

1. Martin, Judith, *Miss Manners' Guide to Excruciatingly Correct Behavior,* New York: Atheneum, 1982, pp. 572 - 578.

2. Hamm, Madeleine McDermott, "His & Hers: Furniture from 2 Households," *Houston Chronicle* (October 14, 1989), p. 1D.

3. *Webster's New Twentieth Century Dictionary of The English Language, 2nd ed.,* New York: Simon and Schuster, 1983, p. 194.

Chapter 3

1. Cherlin, Andrew, *Marriage, Divorce, Remarriage,* Cambridge, Massachusetts: Harvard University Press, 1981, pp. 87 - 89.

Chapter 4

1. Hunt, Morton, "When Little Things Go Wrong," *Parade Magazine,* June 11, 1989, pp. 8 - 10.

2. Visher, Emily B., Ph.D. and John S. Visher, M.D., *Stepfamilies: A Guide to Working with Stepparents and Stepchildren,* Secaucus, New Jersey: The Citadel Press, 1979, p. 139.

Chapter 5

1. For example: "Ann Landers," *Houston Chronicle,* July 28, 1989, p. 2E.

2. Mann, Thomas H., *Differences in Children's Aggressiveness in Stepfather Families and Nondivorced Families,* master's thesis, University of Houston, Spring, 1987, p. 54.

3. White, Lynn K. and Alan Booth, "The Quality and Stability of Remarriages: The Role of Stepchildren," *American Sociological Review,* Vol. 50 (October 1985), p. 693.

Chapter 6
1. Thies, Jill Matthews, "Beyond Divorce: The Impact of Remarriage on Children," *Journal of Clinical Child Psychology,* Vol 6 (2, Summer 1977), p. 60.

Chapter 8
1. Dowling, Claudia, "The Relative Explosion", *Psychology Today,* Vol 17 (4, April 1983), p. 58.

Chapter 9
Much of the material in this Chapter is based on:
Saltzman, Earl S. Ph.D., *Structured Discipline Communication,* Houston, Texas: Saltzman Center For Family Relationships, 1979.

Chapter 10
1. Fromm, Erich, *The Art of Loving,* New York: Harper & Row, 1974, pp. 4 - 5.

2. Berman, Claire, *Adult Children of Divorce Speak Out,* New York, Simon & Schuster, 1991, p. 175.

3. Ibid., pp. 177 - 179.

4. "The Rose" (Amanda McBroom), used by permission.

Books by Starburst Publishers
(Partial listing—full list available on request)

The New American Family —Artlip, Artlip, & Saltzman
American men and women are remarrying at an astounding rate, and nearly 60% of the remarriages involve children under the age of eighteen. Unfortunately, over half of these remarriages also end in divorce, with half of the "redivorces" occuring within five years. The New American Family tells it like it is. It gives examples and personal experiences that help you to see that the second time around is no picnic. It provides practical, good sense suggestions and guidelines for making your new American family the one you always dreamed of.

(trade paper)   ISBN 0914984446   **$10.95**

Dragon Slaying For Parents —Tom Prinz
Subtitled: Removing The Excess Baggage So You Can Be The Parent You Want To Be. Shows how Dragons such as Codependency, Low Self-Esteem and other hidden factors interfere with effective parenting. This book by a marriage, family, and child counselor, is for all parents—to assist them with the difficult task of raising responsible and confident children in the 1990's. It is written especially for parents who believe they have "tried everything!"

(trade paper)   ISBN 0914984357   **$9.95**

Man And Wife For Life —Joseph Kanzlemar
A penetrating and often humorous look into real life situations of married people. Helps the reader get a new understanding of the problems and relationships within marriage.

(trade paper)   ISBN 0914984233   **$7.95**

Alzheimer's—Does "The System" Care?   —Ted & Paula Valenti
Experts consider Alzheimer's disease to be the "disease of the century." More than half the one million elderly people residing in American nursing homes have "senile dementia." This book reveals a unique observation as to the cause of Alzheimer's and the care of its victims.

(hard cover)   ISBN 0914984179   **$14.95**

What To Do When The Bill Collector Calls! —David L. Kelcher, Jr.

Reveals the unfair debt collection practices that some agencies use and how this has led to the invasion of privacy, bankruptcy, marital instability, and the loss of jobs. This is a ready reference guide that tells the reader what he can do about the problem.

(trade paper) ISBN 0914984322 **$9.95**

You Can Eliminate Stress From The I.R.S. —Fulton N. Dobson

Almost everyone can expect to undergo a tax audit at least once or twice in their lifetime. This book gives common sense actions to take that will make the audit easier to face. Answers questions like: What are my rights as a taxpayer? What can I expect from my tax accountant? How can I prove to the IRS my ability (or inability) to pay back taxes? . . . and much more.

(trade paper) ISBN 0914984403 **$7.95**

Like A Bulging Wall —Robert Borrud

Will you survive the 1990's economic crash? This book shows how debt, greed, and covetousness, along with a lifestyle beyond our means, has brought about an explosive situation in this country. Gives "call" from God to prepare for judgement in America. Also lists TOP-RATED U.S. BANKS and SAVINGS & LOANS.

(trade paper) ISBN 0914984284 **$8.95**

The Quick Job Hunt Guide —Robert D. Siedle

Gives techniques to use when looking for a job. Networking, Following the Ten-Day Plan, and Avoiding the Personnel Department, are some of the ways to "land that job!"

(trade paper) ISBN 0914984330 **$7.95**

Get Rich Slowly . . . But Surely! —Randy L. Thurman

The only get-rich-quick guide you'll ever need. Achieving financial independence is important to young and old. Anyone who wants to be financially free will discover the way to financial independence easier by applying these long-term, time-tested principles. This book can be read in one sitting!

(trade paper) ISBN 0914984365 **$7.95**

Allergy Cooking With Ease —Nicolette N. Dumke

A book designed to provide a wide variety of recipes to meet many different types of dietary and social needs, and, whenever possible, save you time in food preparation. Includes: Recipes for those special foods that most food allergy patients think they will never eat again; Timesaving tricks; and Allergen Avoidance Index.

(trade paper-opens flat) ISBN 091498442X **$12.95**

The Low-Fat Supermarket   —Judith & Scott Smith

A comprehensive reference of over 4,500 brand name products that derive less than 30% of their calories form fat. Information provided includes total calories, fat, cholesterol and sodium content. Organized according to the the sections of a supermarket. Your answer to a healthier you.

(trade paper)   ISBN 0914984438   **$10.95**

Purchasing Information

<u>Listed books are available from your favorite Bookstore,</u> either from current stock or special order. To assist bookstore in locating your selection be sure to give title, author, and ISBN #. If unable to purchase from the bookstore you may order direct from STARBURST PUBLISHERS. When ordering enclose full payment plus $2.00* for shipping and handling ($2.50* if Canada or Overseas). Payment in US Funds only. Please allow two to three weeks minimum (longer overseas) for delivery. Make checks payable to and mail to STARBURST PUBLISHERS, P.O. Box 4123, LANCASTER, PA 17604. **Prices subject to change without notice.** Catalog available upon request.

*We reserve the right to ship your order the least expensive way. If you desire first class (domestic) or air shipment (overseas) please enclose shpping funds as follows: First Class within the USA enclose $4.00, Airmail Canada enclose $5.00, and Overseas enclose 30% (minimum $5.00) of total order. All remittance must be in US Funds.　　　　　　　　　　　　　　　　　　　　　11-92

DIED IN THE WOOL